D0746694

"It is in the importer's best interest to research each import before actually placing a purchase order, so as to be sure that he is capable of importing the product legally and then being able to sell it for a profit."

- Rich Pencak

A Complete Yet Concise Guide to

Importing
Purchases into
These United
States of
America

Compiled and written by
Richard J. Pencak
United States Customhouse Broker
Associate Adjunct Professor, International Trade, New York University
Author, "Common Sense Importing"

1999

FIRST EDITION

Printed in the United States of America

Copyright © 1999 Rich Pencak

APPRECIATION

It is with great appreciation that I commend Lynn DuHoffman and Frances Laudicina who both assisted me with editing this endeavor. I thank Sam Zekser, Alex Encanarcion, Peter Klastadt, Dick Stein, and Robert E. Lee (the Customhouse Broker not the General) for their support, both moral and literate. Thanks to Dustin Adams for the covers, and computer work. Many thanks to Joe Cioffi. Kudos to Patrick Pencak and Johann DuHoffman for always making me feel 20 years younger. Always thanks to my parents, Charles and Harriett Pencak. Special thanks to Patricia Pencak for putting up with me for the last quarter century.

My thanks also to the U.S. Customs service who have generously given their permission for me to reprint forms used in their training manual. These forms can be found in the Appendix.

DISCLAIMER

This is a guide and just that. As indicated herein, before finalizing any import, experts should be consulted and the reader should not rely upon this book as their only reference book. The writer does not intend it to be the final source but a practical guide to find the answers.

Note that terms of sale used in this book have historically been used for decades, and for the most part still are used instead of the recently created Incoterms. Readers are encouraged to contact the International Chamber of Commerce for Incoterms.

Contents

Page

Preface & Disclaimer

PREFACE

For the novice or first time importer
Have you ever thought about international buying for your business but felt the topic too overwhelming? Have you heard too many horror stories from people who currently import? That's because it is never taught in high schools, and business classes only delve into the theories of international trade. For a decade I have lectured at New York University. I learned what questions needed to be answered from the students and each year geared the class more and more to the needs of the students.

I have learned that the incredible fast pace of modern society leaves few individuals with the time or inclination to learn all that there is about international trade. Who has time for a 500-page book. Hire a professional! Specialists in the field, be they U.S. Customs employees, Customhouse Brokers, or Freight Forwarders can be used to their full potential if the importer knows the right questions and basic principles.

For the already active importer
While many basic points are already known to the veteran importer, it is difficult for anyone, this writer included, to be aware of the total field of international trade. Importing to the U.S. is so complex that I am certain I can still learn shortcuts and information from importers about specific products, that I lack familiarity with. Perhaps there is information that I have learned and have since forgotten over the last few decades?

Knowledgeable importers can still use this book as a training tool to employees new to international trade. This writer concedes that every topic is not discussed herein, however, there are books hundreds of pages long that do not confront the following basic issues:

1. How is an importer sure that he legally can import any product?
2. How does an importer set up a purchase order to his advantage?
3. How to calculate an accurate landed cost, before actually buying.

Each of these crucial questions will be answered, in great detail, in this book. Specifically, the reader is taught how to ASK THE RIGHT QUESTIONS and WHO TO CONTACT FOR THE RIGHT ANSWERS!

CHAPTER ONE

SUMMARY OF IMPORT PROCEDURES

ALWAYS RESEARCH YOUR IMPORT

There are two basic concepts that must always be considered before deciding to purchase goods internationally. They are:

1. *Legality*
Any product, manufacture or growth that you plan to import into the United States must be researched to see if it is legal to import that commodity based on the country of origin, as well as the very nature of the article itself.

2. *Landed Cost*
The cost of buying merchandise from a foreign country MUST be considered in the context of ALL THE ADDITIONAL COSTS THAT MUST BE PAID TO IMPORT THAT CARGO. The final cost to get the cargo to the importer's premise, or his customer's warehouse is known as the landed cost. This cost can (and always should) be calculated on paper, in advance of the actual import. If it seems cost prohibitive, the *"loss"* is only on paper! The importer should not be disheartened, as the following alternatives exist to reduce the landed cost:
   a) Purchase in larger quantities.
   b) Research lower transportation costs.
   c) Ship by ocean freight instead of air freight.
   d) Negotiate a better price from the foreign vendor.
   e) Find a vendor with more competitive prices.

THE CUSTOMS ENTRY

All cargo arriving into the United States, by any mode, needs to be cleared through U.S. Customs. The forms filed with Customs to obtain this clearance are known as the "entry." Items valued under $2000.00 and not trade sensitive (textile products for example) can be cleared as an **"informal entry"** directly with Customs by the importer. Higher values and trade-sensitive items of any value require **"formal entry."** While importers are allowed to clear their own cargo, the intelligent option is to hire a **"Customhouse Broker."**

MODES OF TRANSPORT

Cargo can arrive in the United States by various modes of transport. Which mode importers choose to use is limited by the size and weight (couriers, mail and planes have limits) or logistics (only truck and trains can arrive from Mexico or Canada).

1. *Mail*
Mail is restricted by the size of the package and the weight. These limitations vary on a country-by-country basis, and can be researched by contacting the consular of the country of export. Shipping by mail is slow but usually inexpensive when compared to couriers and airfreight. Registered postal services are very dependable. If an informal entry is allowed, the postman delivers the goods to the consignee, and any Customs duties collected as a C.O.D. Formal entries generally require a Customhouse Broker along with the additional expense. Importers shipping low values of non-restricted goods should be careful not to ask the foreign seller to ship too many separate shipments one or two days apart. Or they can be combined by U.S. Customs if they arrive in the Unites States at the same time, resulting in the costs of a formal entry. However, it is not legal to break down large cargoes into small mail parcels to intentionally avoid formal entry.

2. *Courier*
Couriers promise a day or two service from overseas and offer door-to-door service. With sample and priority shipments they are very convenient, but often costly. Most couriers have an 800- phone number, offering rates as well as maximum size and weights per package.

3. *Rail and Truck*
These can only be used to the United States when shipping from Canada or Mexico. Carriers should be chosen who can transport the cargo directly into the United States, and not have to drop the cargo at the border, creating additional warehouse expense. These carriers usually work with a Customhouse Broker at the border who can either make entry or ship **"in-bond"** (this allows the freight to travel without being cleared, within the United States) to any Customs location further inland.

4. *Ocean Freight*
The most economical way of transporting commercial cargo.

5. *Air Freight*
A fast way to ship goods, but costly. Importers will continually compare the speed of airfreight with the savings of ocean freight.

6. *Excess Baggage*
Much cheaper than airfreight, this mode of transport does require the importer or his counterpart to travel with the goods. The amount of excess baggage can be limited by the airline, based on the combined weight of the passengers and their luggage. Often airlines are completely booked, especially around Christmas and Easter. The importer of large excess baggage shipments should be prepared to have some of the cargo left at points of transfer, so a direct airline flight is recommended.

WHAT DETAILS TO FIND OUT FROM THE VENDOR

An important factor to always find out from your foreign vendor, along with his original offered price and terms of sale, is how the goods are packed, so that they can be shipped internationally. Usually, the packing is included in the cost of the cargo. If it is not, find out how much the additional cost will be. The exact dimensions of each outer carton, as well as the gross weight is essential to calculate the landed cost. If the landed cost leaves enough room to sell the product with a profitable margin, or is lower than the goods can be purchased domestically in the United States then the actual import may be carefully undertaken.

Often a sample, or test shipment is ordered before an investment is placed in a large order. The importer or an independent testing company representing the importer should test items. The quality shown in the sample should be recorded and used as a factor to test samples from the commercial order, when and if it is placed.

Issuing a purchase order notifies the seller of the importer's intention to purchase the merchandise. All details MUST be worked out in advance of issuing the purchase order, such as research with U.S. Customs and all other government agencies (see page 19), freight, insurance and all other costs (see page 37).

HOW CARGO IS SHIPPED INTERNATIONALLY

Buying internationally offers challenges to the buyer that he is not faced with when purchasing within the United States. The importer must be concerned that once he pays for merchandise he will receive it. The seller is concerned that he will send cargo to the United States and never get paid. Unless a long-term relationship exists between the vendor and buyer, 60-day remittance terms are **unheard of**. To resolve these issues, international shipping laws mandate that the bill of lading (or air waybill), once issued by a carrier or bonded forwarder will grant legal title of the cargo. The bill of lading can be compared to a coat check, which is given to the seller after the cargo ships by the freight forwarder. The bill of lading must be presented to the freight forwarder's office in the United States in order to reclaim the cargo.

An international freight forwarder usually issues documentation and coordinates shipping in the foreign country, acting as an intermediary between the trucker, shipping company, piers, terminals and Customs (overseas). In some instances, Customs entry must be made in both the exporting country and upon arrival in the United States. Any required documentation (see page 66) is then either sent through banking channels (when the goods are purchased on a letter of credit) or directly to the importer. Most documents are sent by courier to the United States.

As the seller relies upon the overseas freight forwarder to coordinate the shipping of the cargo and to be certain all export documentation is prepared correctly and filed timely, the importer relies upon his Customhouse Broker at the location of arrival to make entry on his behalf. The Broker satisfies U.S. Custom's as well as any other Federal or State agency, obtains the release from the carrier or freight forwarder and issues domestic trucking instructions to have the cargo delivered to its final destination. To accomplish these tasks it is the importer's obligation to be sure that

1. The broker is aware of when and how the cargo is shipped.
2. The broker gets all the necessary documents in advance of the arrival of the cargo.

When cargo arrives in the United States the importer has a choice of the type of entry to make. A consumption entry releases the cargo from Customs custody. A warehouse entry places the cargo, after clearance, in a bonded warehouse in the U.S. without payment of U.S. duties. Most entries can be filed up to five days in advance of arrival. U.S. Customs then notifies the importer if the cargo is released with or without an examination. Certain restricted merchandise, such as quota shipments, requires all Customs formalities completed before the release of the cargo.

CLEARING CUSTOMS AND SATISFYING THE SHIPPING AGENT OR CARRIER MUST BE VIEWED AS TWO SIDES OF THE SAME COIN. BOTH HAVE TO BE SATISFIED. WHEN ONE IS NOT, THE CARGO CANNOT LEAVE THE PIER OR TERMINAL OF ARRIVAL!

THE IMPORTER'S RESPONSIBILITIES

1. The importer must provide his Customhouse Broker with the original air waybill or bill of lading, commercial invoice from the seller, packing list and another special documentation that might be required for the Customhouse Broker to make entry and obtain clearance of the cargo. To accomplish this, he must be certain that his overseas seller first fax copies of the documents at time of shipment and then follow up with the original documents in advance of the arrival of the cargo. For air shipments, the original documents generally accompany the cargo. With ocean shipments the foreign vendor (at the importer's expense) usually sends the documents via courier.

2. The importer must provide his Customhouse Broker with a valid Power of Attorney so that the broker may legally act on his behalf. Although the importer uses a Customhouse Broker to clear cargo, he still must be reasonably proficient in his understanding of basic Customs rules and regulations.

3. The importer must be certain that the information provided to Customs on any documentation is accurate and complete. Often the importer must furnish the seller with all details on how to comply with Customs regulations.

4. The importer is responsible for any freight costs that are collected, Customs duties and fees, as well as paying the Customhouse Broker his fee.

5. It is in the importer's best interest to research each import **before actually placing a purchase order,** so as to be sure that he is capable of importing the product legally and then being able to sell it for a profit.

CAN ANYONE IMPORT? IS A LICENSE TO IMPORT REQUIRED?

The United States allows anyone or any company to import goods into the United States. Registration with U.S. Customs is essential, but not difficult, and is usually filed by the Customhouse Broker. The registration requires a legal address, as well as social security number (individual), or federal tax ID number (corporations). If the importer does not have either number, Customs will assign a "temporary" number for the importer to use.

Additional license requirements are called for when other Federal agencies such as the Department of Agriculture, Bureau of Alcohol, Tobacco and Firearms or the Department of Fish and Wildlife (to name a few) require the importer to obtain a license to import products requiring review and release by their agency (refer to page 19).

CARNETS

Carnets are a unique combination of an entry and bond. They are used primarily by salesman who intend to travel from country to country with the intention of eventually returning to the originating nation with the samples intact. For import shipments to the United States under a carnet, the vendor obtains the carnet by posting a cash deposit with an international carnet office as well as registering with required statistical information. The samples covered by the carnet are permitted rapid Customs entry with minimum formalities in each country that they are sent. More information concerning carnets are available from-

United States Council for International Business- <u>Carnet Office</u>
1212 Avenue of the Americas at 47th Street (18th Floor)
New York, N. Y. 10036
Tel- (212) 354-4480   Fax- (212) 944-0012
info@uscib.org.   http://www.us.cib.org

FOREIGN TRADE ZONE

Imported cargo can be placed in a FTZ upon arrival into the United States. An FTZ is a special region that is, technically speaking, not considered part of the United States ("foreign" warehouses or localities within the U.S.). When goods leave the Foreign Trade Zone for entry to the U.S. Customs formalities apply again. Inside the Trade Zone, merchandise is allowed to be transformed into a new product.

There is a fine line between goods that are placed into a FTZ and goods placed in a bonded warehouse. A bond is not required to place goods into the FTZ and may remain there for an indefinite period of time. Foreign cargo maybe placed into the Foreign Trade Zone and then altered or manufactured to create a different article. Often the importer can achieve a legal savings of duty by having goods manufactured within a trade zone. Any importer contemplating using the FTZ is encouraged to petition Customs with details of their intentions to be certain they are complying with Customs regulations and a savings can indeed be achieved.

MARKING REQUIREMENTS

All merchandise arriving into the United States is required to be marked conspicuously, indelibly, and permanently with the country of origin UNLESS exempted from marking. Please refer to the APPENDIX for a list of exemptions. Common sense prevails in marking requirements. Items too small to be marked are exempted from marking. Importers should always be certain to have their cargo marked overseas if not exempted. Note that even when the article itself is exempted from marking the outside packing STILL REQUIRES MARKING WITH THE COUNTRY OF ORIGIN.

CHAPTER TWO

HOW TO BE CERTAIN YOU ARE
IMPORTING LEGALLY

Definitions for U.S. CUSTOMS ENTRY-

PROHIBITED: NOT ALLOWED AT ALL!
RESTRICTED: ALLOWED UNDER CERTAIN CONDITIONS!

PROHIBITED CARGO

Sometimes imports are not allowed. They are PROHIBITED. They are banned based on three criterions -

a. The item itself
Some examples, but not all items are certain banned narcotics, ethnographic artifacts, unlawful imports of copyrighted, trademark, patented or trade name products, merchandise that is not approved for import due to hazards to human health or environment, as well as products made from endangered species.

b. The country where it is made, grown or produced
The products, growth or manufacture of certain countries, such as Cuba, Iraq, Iran and Libya are banned from being imported. This includes products of these nations sent through a country not banned. **"JUST SHIPPING THE PRODUCT THROUGH A COUNTRY DOES NOT MAKE THAT ITEM, BY SOME MIRACLE, TRANSFORM ITS IDENTITY INTO A PRODUCT OF THE NEW COUNTRY."**

c. State and local regulations
Importers must be certain all state or local laws are abided by. Some items that should merit attention are- alcohol, tobacco, firearms, gambling devices and narcotics.

THE UNITED STATES CUSTOMS SERVICE

When any importer contemplates an international purchase one of his first phone calls should be to the U.S. CUSTOMS SERVICE. U.S. CUSTOMS freely offers details to any importer, or prospective importer seeking information.

U.S. Customs has 52 central areas known as ports. Ports are often seaports, but can be any location where cargo arrives to be cleared through U.S. Customs. This includes seaports, airports as well as major highway routes into the United States. The importer should contact the port where he intends to have his cargo cleared through Customs or if this location is not known, the closest port. A list of Customs ports follows:

U.S. CUSTOMS PORTS

Port of Anchorage
605 W. Fourth Avenue
Anchorage, Alaska 99501
Phone   907 271-2675
Fax   907 271-2684

Port of Nogales
9 Grand Avenue
Nogales, Arizona 85621
Phone   520 287-1410
Fax   520 287-1421

Port of Calexico
P.O. Box 632
Calexico, California 92232
Phone   760 768-2300
Fax   760 768-2301

Port of San Francisco
555 Battery Street
San Francisco, California 94111
Phone   415 782-9200
Fax   415 705-1226

Port of Mobile
150 N. Royal St. Room 3004
Mobile, Alabama 36602
Phone   334 441-5106
Fax   334 441-6061

Port of Tucson
7150 S. Tucson Blvd.
Tucson, Arizona 85706
Phone   520 670-6461
Fax   520 670-6648

Port of Otay Mesa
9777 Via De La Amistad
San Diego, California 92154
Phone   619 661-3305
Fax   619 661-3049

Port of Denver
4735 Oakland Street
Denver, Colorado 80239
Phone   303 371-3014
Fax   303 371-3285

Port of District of Columbia
Dulles Airport PO Box 17423
Washington D.C. 20041
Phone   703 661-3660
Fax   703 318-6706

Port of Miami Seaport
1500 Port Blvd.
Miami, Florida 33132
Phone   305 536-5261
Fax   305 536-4734

Port of Atlanta
700 Doug Davis Drive
Atlanta, Georgia 30354
Phone   404 763-7020
Fax   404 763-7038

Port of Honolulu
335 Merchant Street
Honolulu, Hawaii 96813
Phone   808 522-8060
Fax   808 522-8081

Port of Louisville
601 West Broadway Rt. 45
Louisville, Kentucky 40202
Phone   502 582-5186
Fax   502 625-7224

Port of Portland (Maine)
312 Fore Street
Portland, Maine 04101
Phone   207 771-3600
Fax   207 771-3627

Port of Baltimore
40 South Gay Street
Baltimore, Maryland 21202
Phone   410 962-2666
Fax   410 962-9335

Port of Miami Airport
P.O. Box 52-3215
Miami, Florida 33122
Phone   305 869-2800
Fax   305 869-2822

Port of Tampa
1624 E. 7th Avenue Suite 101
Tampa, Florida 33605
Phone   813 228-2385
Fax   813 228-2508

Port of Savannah
One East Bay Street
Savannah, Georgia 31401
Phone   912 652-4256
Fax   912 652-4435

Port of Chicago
610 S. Canal Street
Chicago, Illinois 60607
Phone   312 983-1100
Fax   312 353-2337

Port of New Orleans
423 Canal Street
New Orleans, Louisiana 70130
Phone   504 670-2391
Fax   504 670-2123

Port of Boston
10 Causeway Street
Boston, MA. 02222
Phone   617 565-6147
Fax   617 565-5099

Port of Detroit
477 Michigan Avenue Suite 200
Detroit, Michigan 48226
Phone   313 442-0200
Fax   313 226-3179

Port of Duluth 515 W. First Street # 209 Duluth, Minnesota 55802 Phone 218 720-5201 Fax 218 720-5216	**Port of Minneapolis/St. Paul** 330 Second Ave. South Suite 560 Minneapolis, Minnesota 55401 Phone 612 348-1669 Fax 612 348-1630
Port of Kansas City 2701 Rock Creek Parkway Suite 202 N. Kansas City, Missouri 64116 Phone 816 374-6439 Fax 816 374-6422	**Port of St. Louis** 4477 Woodson Road St. Louis, Missouri 63134 Phone 314 428-2662 Fax 314 428-2889
Port of Great Falls 300 2nd Avenue South Great Falls, Montana 59405 Phone 406 453-7631 Fax 406 453-7069	**Port of Charlotte** 1901 Cross Beam Drive Charlotte, North Carolina 28217 Phone 704 329-6100 Fax 704 329-6103
Port of Pembina PO Box 610 Pembina, North Dakota 58271 Phone 701 825-6813 Fax 701 825-6953	**Port of Newark** 1210 Corbin Street Elizabeth, New Jersey 07201 Phone 201 443-0100 Phone 201 443-0550
Port of Buffalo 111 W. Huron Street Buffalo, New York 14202 Phone 716 551-5200 Fax 716 551-5011	**Port of Champlain** 198 W. Service Road Champlain, New York 12919 Phone 518 298-8327 Fax 518 298-8315
Port of New York 6 World Trade Center New York, New York 10048 Phone 212 637-7900 Fax 212 637-7944	**Port of JFK Airport** Building 77 JFK Airport Jamaica, New York 11430 Phone 718 553-1542 Fax 718 553-0077
Port of Cleveland 6747 Engle Road Middlebury Heights, Ohio 44130 Phone 440 891-3800 Fax 440 891-3836	**Port of Portland (Oregon)** 8337 NE Alderwood Rd. Rm 200 Portland Oregon 97220 Phone 503 326-7625 Fax 503 326-7629

Port of Philadelphia
2nd & Chestnut Streets
Philadelphia, Pennsylvania 19106
Phone 215 597-4606
Fax   215 597-8370

Port of San Juan
#1 La Puntilla Street
San Juan, Puerto Rico 00901
Phone 787 729-6850
Fax   787 729-6678

Port of Dallas/Fort Worth
P.O. Box 619050
Dallas/Fort Worth Airport, Texas 75261
Phone 972 574-2170
Fax   972 574-4818

Port of Houston/Galveston
2350 N. Sam Houston Pkwy E. Suite 1000
Houston, Texas 77032
Phone 281 985-6712
Fax   281 985-6706

Port of Norfolk
200 Granby Street
Norfolk, VA 23510
Phone 757 441-3400
Fax   757 441-6630

Port of Christiansted
P.O. Box 249
St. Croix. Virgin Is. 00821
Phone 340 773-1490
Fax   340 778-7419

Port of Blaine
9901 Pacific Highway
Blaine, Washington 98230
Phone 360 332-5771
Fax   360 332-4701

Port of Providence
49 Pavilion Avenue
Providence, Rhode Island 02905
Phone 401 941-6326
Fax   401 941-6628

Port of Charleston
200 E. Bay Street
Charleston, South Carolina 29401
Phone 843 727-4157
Fax   843 727-4501

Port of El Paso
797 S. Saragosa Road
El Paso, Texas 79907
Phone 915 872-3407
Fax   915 872-3412

Port of Laredo/Columbia
PO Box 3130
Laredo, Texas 78044
Phone 956 726-2267
Fax   956 726-2948

Port of Charlotte/Amalie V.I.
Main Post Office - Sugar Estate
St. Thomas, Virgin Islands 00801
Phone 340 774-2510
Fax   340 776-3489

Port of St. Albans
P.O. Box 1490
St. Albans, Vermont 05478
Phone 802 524-6527
Fax   802 527-1338

Port of Seattle
1000 Second Avenue Suite 2100
Seattle, Washington 98104
Phone 206 553-0770
Fax   206 553-2940

Port of Tacoma
2202 Port of Tacoma Road
Tacoma, Washington 98421
Phone 253 593-6336
Fax   253 593-6351

Port of Milwaukee
6269 Ace Industrial Drive
Cudahy, Wisconsin 53110
Phone 414 571-2860
Fax   414 762-0253

When calling U.S. Customs, the importer should ask to speak to **the Commodity Specialist** who is assigned to oversee all imports for the specific product that is being researched. A Commodity Specialist is just that, a specialist, **AN EXPERT.** For example, if the importer is planning on shipping foodstuffs, he should ask to consult with **"The Commodity Specialist for foodstuffs."** Providing information to prospective importers is just one task of the Commodity Specialist, who also reviews and monitors the actual imports for that product line.

The importer should be prepared when calling the Commodity Specialist. He should know all the details of his prospective import including, but not limited to: the factory or location where the product is grown, produced or manufactured. Any trade, alternate or common name the product may be known by, the component material breakdown by weight (example- 50% brass, 35% zinc, 15% steel), what is the product's intended use in the United States and any other revelent information that can be supplied by the manufacturer. The importer should also keep a record, in writing, of whom he is talking with, on what date and all details of the conversation.

I must comment at this time on proper courtesy and protocol. The importer should be constantly aware that they are talking with a respected and knowledgeable official of the United States Customs Service, who is providing the requested information free of charge. If the import matures to fruition, this very Customs official is a person whom the importer will most likely be associating with for the foreseeable future. I urge any importer to be polite and patient, and not to feel affronted if they must wait for a call back, or are told to call back later in the day, or even the next day. U.S. Customs provides this free service to the public for all inquiries, however, active shipments do get priority over inquiries. There is no charge for the information, as U.S. Customs would rather answer an inquiry before the actual import takes place, than have to deny entry because a necessary technicality was needlessly overlooked. Having put this matter into proper prospective, here are the essential Customs' questions that, once answered, will provide the importer with all relevant details to a legal and successful import.

EIGHT ESSENTIAL QUESTIONS TO ASK OF U.S. CUSTOMS

The following eight questions summarize what a potential importer **MUST** ask the U.S. Customs Commodity Specialist they have sought out. The answers will enlighten the importer to the legality of the transaction, what Customs regulations apply to their specific inquiry, which documents are necessary to obtain clearance, if any other government agency's approval is required, as well as many other important issues.

1. Is the item prohibited?
If advised that the item of your proposed import is banned, find an item to import that is not prohibited, or a country whose products are allowed entry.

2. If it is not prohibited, is it restricted? If restricted, how?
Imports can be restricted in various ways. U.S. Customs can monitor any item from any country, thus counting the quantities of each import for possible future trade action. "Restricted" can refer to the item being accountable to a quota, needing special licensing, being trade sensitive, needing special documents or even needing other agency review. "Restricted" means that the importer must carefully note how it is restricted and adhere to all requirements. Restricted items are not allowed informal entry privileges, and can even require all documents to be submitted and verified before release of the cargo.

3. Are any "special" documents needed at time of import?
All entries require a commercial invoice (detailed bill of sale from the seller) packing list, and proof of right to make entry. This proof can be a copy of the bill of lading, airway bill, or carrier certificate. In some cases one or more additional forms or licenses may be required by U.S. Customs. Some documents may be filled out by the Customhouse Broker or importer, some by the seller, and some have to be obtained from various foreign government offices in the country of manufacture or production. Once U.S. Customs advises the need of these special document(s) that must be approved or originate in the country of export, the importer should be certain the seller can provide the same document, hopefully for a cost included in their price.

4. Are there any other government agencies who must approve the import of this product?
Based on the imported product, and its use, other federal agencies may have to be notified of the arrival, and the appropriate documentation filed BEFORE Customs clearance is permitted. U.S. Customs will refer an importer to the agencies who have jurisdiction over that commodity. The importer must then contact these agencies, in advance of the import, to learn of any special requirements, labeling or documentation that is required. Failure to adhere to their import requirements can result in fines, penalties or refused admittance. **DENIED ENTRY IS JUST AS SERIOUS IF ORDERED BY THE FDA, ATF, BAI or U.S. CUSTOMS!**

5. What is the duty rate and classification of the intended import?
All imported items are required to be classified in accordance with the Harmonized Schedule of the United States. This huge listing of over 30,000 items allows Customs and the importer to pinpoint under what tariff number the product should be imported. Each tariff number has a corresponding rate of duty, or reflects duty-free status, based on the country of export. Customs can advise the duty rate over the phone in most cases. This advisory is not legally binding, but usually correct. For the format to request a legally binding ruling see page 18.

6. Are the imported products subject to Countervailing Duty (CVD) or Antidumping Duty (ADD)?
Antidumping duty and countervailing duty are special duties that are added to the usual accessed duty rates to compensate for unfair trade practices of either the manufacturer or the country of export. Only a few hundred items have these additional duties, but if these duties are overlooked the negligent importer can suffer with additional duties as high as 100% of the value. Fear and dread not, some CVD or ADD duties are small (as low as 1%), and in some instances U.S. Customs permits the importer to post a bond in lieu of a cash deposit until the court cases are finalized.

7. Are there any specific marking requirements?
U.S. Customs requires imported goods and their outside packaging to be marked to show the country of origin to the ultimate purchaser, in a manner conspicuous, legible, indelible and in English. In some cases U.S. Customs will require items to be marked in a specific way, such as die-casting (for most tools), sewn in labels (for textile products), or even metal plates (for machines). Hundreds of specific marking requirements exist. If there is no specific marking requirements U.S. Customs usually allows marking with an adhesive sticker (difficult to remove), in a location easily apparent to the ultimate purchaser in the U.S.

8. Is the item subject to quota? If so how?
Quota is a restrictive system that protects specific endangered domestic industries from excessive imports. Limits are placed, usually annually, on the countries whose volume of import for that product is the largest. Absolute quotas when fully subscribed, prohibit further imports until the quota renews the following year. Importers have the unpleasant options of re-exporting, warehousing (until next year) or destruction. Tariff rate quotas, when filled, punish the importer with higher duty rates.

THE IMPORTANCE OF CORRECT CLASSIFICATION

All imports into the United States must be classified in accordance with the "Harmonized Tariff of the United States". This tariff is broken down into 100 chapters, each dealing with a specific item. To correctly classify any product, the supplier must provide a complete description of the item, with details such as chief use and component material breakdown by weight. The following section of one page of the tariff gives an excellent example of the detailed information that must be obtained to properly classify the merchandise.

SEE APPENDIX 1

Being an expert at classification takes years of training and great skill. However, having a basic knowledge of classification is important for two reasons.

1. KNOWLEDGE OF THE CORRECT DUTY RATE

Enables an accurate calculation of the landed cost. Classification is not guesswork. It is determined through the format established in the Harmonized Tariff and by numerous Customs rulings and decisions. *FREIGHT RATES CAN BE NEGOTIATED CUSTOMS DUTY RATES CANNOT!* Get an advisory from U.S. Customs via telephone or submit documents for a binding ruling.

2. TO ADVISE THE FOREIGN SELLER HOW TO DESCRIBE THE PRODUCT ON THE INVOICE!

Once the classification is known, how the description reads in the Harmonized Tariff should also be the manner in which the commercial invoice from the foreign vendor describes the product. U.S. Customs can find little fault with an incomplete description on a invoice, if the description mimics how the item is described in the Harmonized Tariff. Descriptions that are incomplete or incorrect will cause U.S. Customs to exam the cargo, at the importer's expense, to determine how to classify the merchandise. It is much easier to have the seller describe it correctly. While this will certainly reduce some examinations, the importer should not expect never to have their cargo examined.

HOW TO LOCATE or PURCHASE A HARMONIZED TARIFF

Purchase the Harmonized Tariff of the United States from:
U.S. Government Printing Office
THE SUPERINTENDENT OF DOCUMENTS
710 North Capitol Street Washington D.C.
(202) 275-2091

The Tariff can often be found at many public and business related libraries throughout the United States.

To obtain the Code of Federal Regulations (CFR) as it pertains to U.S. Customs as well as other agencies, purchase a copy from the U.S. Government Printing Office or local Federal information bookstores. Regulations may also be downloaded from the internet: http://www.access.gpo.gov/nara/cfr/index.html

THE DIFFICULTY OF CLASSIFICATION
One of the more complex areas of classification is wearing apparel. Two entire chapters are devoted to clothes, one being knit, the other not-knit (woven). Each of these chapters list hundreds of divisions by such topics as gender (male, female, children, baby, unisex), material content by weight (cotton, wool, acrylic, etc.) type (shirt, blouse, jacket), use (sport, dress, etc.). It behooves any importer to research the exact description **AS DESCRIBED IN THE TARIFF.**

SOME INTERESTING FACTS ABOUT CLASSIFICATION AND DUTY RATES
The United States offers a free or reduced rate of duty on specific items from many Third World countries. However, this reduction does not cover every item. Imports such as wearing apparel and footwear, seldom, if ever, have free status. Reduced and free rates of duty are available from most of the Third World; almost all of Africa, the Caribbean, South America, Canada, Mexico, Israel, and most of Eastern Europe and Russia, India, Bangladesh and Pakistan. Western Europe, Japan, Taiwan, China and other highly industrial countries are classified under Most Favored Nation Status and no other reduced trade status.

IMPORTANCE AND FORMAT FOR A BINDING RULING
Verbal advice from a Commodity Specialist is very worthwhile, but not legally binding. A legally binding ruling can be obtained on any product free of charge, by submitting, in the proper form, to U.S. Customs a detailed description of the item, its uses, manufacturer (including address), purchase price, terms of sale and likely domestic selling price. Samples, photographs or detailed drawings should be submitted, when available. Lack of sufficient detail or information will result in the return of the ruling request to the importer for completion. The ruling is usually issued within 30-45 days after all necessary information is submitted, advising the importer of the correct legally binding classification and rate of duty. It is LAW unless revoked, and then offers a 30 day grace period for cargo in transit. The importer should forward the ruling to their Customhouse Broker to attach to each entry. **WHEN ANY DOUBT IN CLASSIFICATION EXISTS, BINDING RULINGS ARE MANDATORY!**

A request for a binding ruling should be in the form of a letter, on the importer's stationery. It can also be written on the importer's behalf by his customhouse broker or attorney. The ruling should be addressed as follows:

Regional Commissioner of Customs- New York Region
Attn: Classification and Ruling Requests
6 World Trade Center
New York, N.Y. 10048

Each request for a ruling must give all pertinent details, including names and addresses of all interested parties (importer & foreign vendor). It must state where and when the importation is likely to take place. Send a sample with the ruling request. If a sample is too large, or not available, photographs and diagrams detailing the item would be acceptable. Include other information such as cost, country or origin, material breakdowns, material-value breakdowns, existing patents (if known), and any other information that is available at the time of submission.

Advise Customs of the intended use of the product. In other words, supply Customs with as much information that you have about the item that you are seeking a ruling on. Remember that if any information is missing Customs will not process the ruling, but send you a request for more details.

In addition, in the body of the request, ask Customs for exactly what, if any, are the required documentation for Customs purposes. After all, lacking the proper documentation would spell the early end to an importation. Should the proposed import be for quota merchandise, ask Customs for details concerning the category number and visa/export license requirements.

U.S. Customs will answer most requests within 30 days. There is no fee for a binding ruling and all importers are encouraged to take advantage of this program.

QUOTA
Many imported items are considered a threat to domestic industry. When our government believes that any U.S. industry may be incapable of competing with imported products one of the following two types of quota is often imposed upon their entry into the United States.

1. Absolute Quota (Quantitative Quota)
This quota limits the quantity of an imported item from any given country(s). It allows a certain quantity of the item to be imported within a given period, usually 6 months or 1 year. Always check with U.S. Customs before importing a product to see if it is subject to quota. When the limit is filled, no imports for consumption are allowed. Goods may be

sent to a bonded warehouse, exported or destroyed. Some examples of absolute quota certain types of the following merchandise:

* Wearing apparel, cloth, fabric, and household goods.
* Wooden clothespins, wine, cheeses, dairy products, and Steel.

2. Tariff Rate Quotas

This quota differs from absolute quota in that it has a dual duty rate structure. The usual, favored-nation rate of duty is in effect up until the quota limit is reached, after which a higher, punitive duty rate must be paid. While absolute quota items bar their import during the quota period if the quantity allowed has been reached, the tariff rate quota allows entry under a substantially higher duty rate. Some items covered by tariff rate quota are:

* Fruit juices
* Certain fish and fish products
* Certain dairy products

Basic Quota Precautions

While importing any product requires patient and reliable research, importing goods subject to quota requires special cautions. It is advisable to work with a Customhouse Broker who is familiar with the quota entry processing, as well as an ABI (Automated Broker Interface) broker. If you file quota entries with a non-ABI broker, duty must be paid at time of filing the entry, whereas if the Customhouse Broker is ABI, and he or the importer has ACH (Automated Clearing House, which literally means paying duties with pre-authorized direct bank withdrawals to U.S. Customs), the importer has 10 working days to pay these charges, granting the importer a two week cash flow. Using a Customhouse Broker experienced with quota entries is a mandatory requirement for any importer, as errors at time of entry can result in a closed out quota category.

Before deciding to import any quota item, statistics of the previous year(s) quota usage should be studied and compared to the usage and total allowed import quantity for the current year. Usually, these records can serve as a guide as to when to import the cargo without fear of quota closure. However, be certain to take into account any changes in market demand, for example, about 5 years ago quota linen apparel from China was oversubscribed in the first few months of the year when previously the year's quota allotment was never even filled!

Never import quota merchandise when there is the possibility of the category closing. The combined cost of warehousing or re-exporting merchandise that is shut-out of a quota, as well as the potential loss of customers, delegate international traders of quota merchandise automatically to the top of a high risk category.

CHAPTER THREE

WORKING WITH
OTHER GOVERNMENT AGENCIES
(BESIDES THE U.S. CUSTOMS SERVICE)

In addition to its own responsibilities, U.S. Customs will always check at time of entry, if any other Federal agencies that have an interest in the products being imported have been contacted and clearance allowed. U.S. Customs will not allow entry until all concerned agencies grant their approval. For many entries, no other bureau may have an interest. Other times two or more agencies approval may be required.

THREE VITAL QUESTIONS TO ASK GOVERNMENTAL AGENCIES
Customs can advise if a product must be reviewed by another agency. After this referral, an import compliance officer must be contacted at *EACH* agency. The following is a guideline of questions to ask. Often an import compliance officer will handle the following inquiries:

1. Do I need a license to import this product?
If the answer is yes, ask the person to fax or mail you the application, or tell you how you get it.

2. Do I need any special documentation?
Sometimes, an original document from the country of production must accompany all entry paperwork. Registration of the product or manufacturer may be required by the importer before the actual arrival of the cargo.

3. Do I need any special marking on the packaging?
In many cases, agencies have their own marking requirements, besides U.S. Customs country of origin requirement.

LISTING OF U.S. GOVERNMENT AGENCIES

FOOD AND DRUG ADMINISTRATION (FDA)

Import information- http://www.fda.gov/ora/import/ora_import_program.html
Overview-   http://www.fda.gov/ora/import/ora_import_system.html
Import alerts-   http://www.fda.gov/ora/fiars/ora_import_alert_list.html

For general information, to obtain forms, or information concerning, radiation control standards, Drug and Device Listing and Establishment Registration

Food and Drug Administration
Center for Devices & Radiological Health
Division of Small Manufacturers Assistance
HFZ 220 5600 Fisher's Lane
Rockville, MD 20857
800-638-2041

The following list details many of the products covered by the FDA. IT IS NOT INCLUSIVE. Never take it for granted, when confronted with an import that **"might"** be subject to FDA review because it is not. ALWAYS DOUBLE-CHECK when in doubt. All foods and drinks, utensils used to prepare, consume or serve foods, many chemical products (check on each one), medical devices (thermometers, iron lungs) and machines (including eyeglasses), surgical and food handler gloves, plus many laboratory items and devices are all subject to FDA approval.

When an entry needs review by the FDA, the Customhouse Broker files a notice of arrival with the FDA (FDA701). This form indicates all statistical information about the shipment such as: importer, manufacturer, arrival information and the product. Once notified, the FDA will usually give approval to move the freight from the pier or airport of arrival, to the importer's premise that is within a 50 mile radius of U.S. Customs port of entry (this radius can be extended with FDA approval). The release to premise is NOT a release to sell or use the imported product. It only allows the importer move it from the pier or terminal to avoid costly storage charges. About one week later, the FDA advises their determination to-

a). Release the cargo to the importer for sale or use. No samples, no tests.
b). Sample the product. FDA Inspectors can secure samples directly from the pier, or obtain them by visiting the consignee's warehouse.
c). Order the importer to have the item independently tested. This is known as a documentary sample. The results are forwarded to the FDA.

After reviewing the results of all tests, the FDA then decides to-

a). Release- The importer can use or resell the product.
b). Refused admittance. The importer has 30 days to re-export or destroy the entire shipment under Customs supervision. Duties already paid are refunded only if the cargo is exported under Customs supervision; refund is made without drawback. Failure to export with proper Customs procedures can result in heavy fines as the FDA considers the cargo still in the United States, only exports supervised by customs are considered exported.
c). Refused, but the importer is allowed to:
    i.) Re-process and bring up to standard.
    ii.) Re-label as an inferior product of the quality revealed in the tests. For example, refused medical gloves can, with permission, be re-labeled as industrial gloves and sold as such.

If the FDA denies entry and they do not allow reconditioning or re-labeling, no second chance is given. The standards and criteria upon which the testing is based are public record. The importer can have the same quality tests performed overseas before shipping for consumption in the U.S. However, passing the independent test has no bearing if the product fails the FDA test. It is a precaution that an importer can use to have an indication of the result. Testing for meeting the standards set by the FDA. One condition of the purchase order or letter of credit will be to request a statement from the independent agency, that each product has been tested and approved.

The FDA requires all food items to be labeled with the ingredients in descending order of material content, as well as nutritional and fat guidelines. All labels must be in English. Also, some requirements call for the items only to be sold in specific weights. Importers are advised to have a label printed in advance of packaging, and send it to the FDA for pre-approval, to avoid the unpleasantness of having to re-label the product after arrival.

Overseas manufacturers of medical devices, as well as foreign canning establishments, must pre-register themselves with the FDA. Importers of medical devices must register themselves with the FDA as such.

BUREAU OF AGRICULTURE INSPECTION (BAI) has many divisions-
http://www.aphis.usda.gov/oa/imex.html
Phone- (301) 734-8892

Foreign Agricultural Service
http://fas.usda.gov/itp/imports/usdairy.html

United States Department of Agriculture
Foreign Agricultural Service
Stop 1021, 1400 Independence Avenue
SW Washington, D.C. 20250-1021
202 720-2916

Many cheeses and dairy products imported into the U.S. require a license and are subject to import quotas. Before attempting any such import, contact the phone number above, indicating type of dairy product and origin, as well as manufacturer and manufacturing process. This should be done well in advance of the import.

Food Safety and Quality Service
202 720-1301
http://www.fas.usda.gov/itp/ofsts/ofsts.html

Certain food substances, such as fresh tomatoes, avocados, mangoes, limes, oranges, grapefruits, green peppers, potatoes (certain ones), cucumbers, eggplants, dry onions, walnuts, filberts, processed dates, prunes and olives in tins have to be imported in accordance with grade, size, quality and maturity specifications. Once again, the above telephone number should be contacted to verify any special regulations or licenses needed.

Animal and Plant Health Inspection Services
Import of Live Animals download forms.
http://aphisweb.aphis.usda.gov/forms/index.html#VS16

Main office phone numbers-	(301) 734-6799, 6653, 8891, 6553, 6799
Permit office -	(301) 734-7649
Plant Import Office-	(301) 734-7211
Inspection, Quarantine Facilities-	(301) 734-7612
Living Plant Materials & Products-	(301) 734-8645
Soil, mud, clay, etc.	(301) 734-8393
Livestock	(301) 734-8170

This branch has authority over a wide range of imported articles, such as
a). Fruits, vegetables and nuts.
b). Insects: Not that importing insects is big business, but snails like marble, bugs like tree bark, brass attracts bugs, etc. Bugs are not allowed into the U.S. Items with such infestation require fumigation at the importer's expense.
c). Livestock and domestic animals.

d). Animal byproducts such as hides and skins, wool, hair, bones, meal, etc.

e). Hay and straw. HAY AND/OR STRAW are prohibited. Be certain that your supplier does not use HAY AND/OR STRAW in packing. If found, all the goods must be unpacked, repacked with acceptable packing material and the hay and straw disposed of via incineration. The cost can go into the $1000's!

f). Meat and meat products have their own "meat inspection unit." All meat imported in tins and cans are subject to sampling and incubation to determine shelf stability. Usually 10 -12 cans are taken, mandating that large orders be placed when buying any type of meat product. Meat also requires special marking and grading. Special veterinary certificates are often required from the Animal and Veterinary office of the originating country. Should these certificates be issued incorrectly, even minutely, they will not be accepted and the shipment will be refused admission.

g). Plant and Plant products. All plant imports must be free from dirt, and shipped with the roots "dirt free." Dirt is also a prohibited import.

h). Poultry and poultry products. In addition to being subject to the standard meat inspection regulations, poultry may require additional licensing.

i). Biological drugs, vaccines intended for animals.

j). Animal feed, be it for livestock or domesticated animals.

k). Pets, such as birds, dogs, monkeys, etc. Be certain, before importing any pet, if a quarantine period is required. Arrangements must be made prior to any importation at the quarantine facility, which is often booked for months in advance. If full, the pet must be shipped to another port or re-exported until room is available. Inquiries about pet imports should be directed to:

Veterinary Services of the Animal Health Inspection Services,
USDA APHIS-US
4700 River Road Riverdale, Maryland. 20737
Phone 301 734 5097
http://www.aphis.usda.gov/NCIE/

Don't forget, for rare fish, monkeys and exotic species, also consult with a representative of the Fish and Wildlife Service, as well as the Veterinary Services Department.

BUREAU OF ALCOHOL, TOBACCO AND FIREARMS (AT&F)

Arms, ammunition, explosives, implements of war

Entry prohibited, unless a license is issued by the AT&F. I suggest anyone interested in importing any of these products, including, but not limited, to a personal hunting or hand gun should hire someone who is a Federal Licensed Gun Dealer and Importer. Any fee charged by the dealer is deminimus compared to the time and money needed to get a license. In addition to the AT&F, with reference to these explosive devices, it may be necessary to contact-

Firearms & Explosives Imports- Bureau of Alcohol, Tobacco and Firearms
650 Massachusetts Avenue Room 5303
NW Washington DC. 20226
http://www.atf.treas.gov/core/firearms/firearms.htm

    Office of Munitions Control   Phone- (703) 875-6644
    For temporary importation, in-transit moves, as well as exportation of arms, a license must be issued before clearance by this Division.

Alcoholic Beverages **(Phone- 202 927-8110 Fax- 202 927-8605)**
Alcohol Import-Export Branch - Bureau ATF
 650 Massachusetts Avenue Room 540 NW
Washington D.C. 20226
http://www.atf.treas.gov/core/alcohol/alcohol.htm

Application for Basic Permit Under the Federal Alcohol Act
http://www.atf.treas.gov/form/form.htm

Assignments for Label Approval of Alcoholic Beverages

C,D,F,Q,T,Z	Marsha Heath	202 927-8099
G,J,L,M,X	Brenda Newton	202 927-8103
H,O,P,R,U,V	Sarah Johnson	202 927-8109
A,B,E,I,N	Dee Dee Foster	202 927-8114
K,S,W,Y	Sherry Zacharias	202 927-8098

NOTE: Due to personnel turn over, these names and assignments will change.
Import Requirements for Various Countries for Beer, Wine & Distilled Spirits
http://www.atf.treas.gov/core/alcohol/info/HOME1.html

Imports for Personal Use
http://www.atf.treas.gov/core/alcohol/info/persimp.htm

Imports for Resale
http://www.atf.treas.gov/core/alcohol/info/impreq.htm
Except for personal use, importers of alcoholic beverages must obtain a basic importer's permit from the AT&F. The importer should also be warned that the basic permit covers only the import of the product, and that at time of entry proof of local and/or state licensing for storage be provided. Also, to transport alcohol, the trucking company must be bonded to handle alcohol.

24

After obtaining the basic importer's permit, the importer must also contend with the following additional regulations.

a). Red Strip Seals- for "hard liquor" these red-strip seals must be attached as a seal over the bottle top. They are purchased by the importer and shipped overseas to be affixed. Customs will verify their presence. Also, the broker should attach a red-strip seal form to the entry.

b). Label Approval- All alcohol bottle labels must be pre-approved by the AT&F. All liquor must be imported in standard sizes, (.375L, .750L, 1L 1.5L, 3L, etc.) Label approvals must be handled well in advance of arrival, as the process is known to take up to six months.

Personal shipments of alcohol, while not prohibited are substantially restricted. The importer must prove to the AT&F that the planned import is to be stored on his premise, and consumed by his household. Before import, a permit must be obtained from the AT&F to import personal liquor and the importer is warned about importing the alcohol ahead of time without the permit.

Tobacco- (800) 398-2282
The AT&F monitor tobacco products of all kinds. Packaging and grading is all subject to AT&F requirements. Importers are encouraged to send labels to confirm compliance with all regulations.

THE FEDERAL TRADE COMMISSION Phone- (202) 326-2222
Makes sure foreign goods are manufactured in accordance with U.S. criteria, such as energy and safety. Most common household appliances are regulated by this commission, such as refrigerators, freezers, and dishwashers.

Consumer Products Efficiency Branch   Phone- (202) 586-1539
To conserve energy, all appliances and consumer goods must alert the consumer to the amount of energy that is consumed during operation, to offer a comparison of annual fuel (electric, gas) costs.

The U.S. Consumer Products Safety Commission Phone- (800) 638-2772
Guards the public from unsafe merchandise, chiefly flammable fabrics. They also safeguard items for children and babies.

Textile Products, Wool and Fur Products
The following marking regulations are **in addition** to the country of origin marking regulation required by U.S. Customs.

Textile Products

1). Fiber content. The public must be informed of the material content of the items by weight (such as 100% cotton, 80% polyester 20% cotton, etc).

2). One of the 3 following options-
   a). The name of the importer
   b). The name of the exporter or foreign vendor
   c). A RN# (REGISTERED NUMBER). A registered number can be obtained from the Federal Trade Commission in Los Angeles.
Phone- (877) 382-4357. A RN# is commonly used so as not to reveal either the importer or seller to the buying public.

3). The country of origin.
The FTC sets exact standards for location, placement and size of this information on garments. For example, all must appear on the main label, in English, large enough to be easily read, and in a specific location depending on the garment. On shirts, the label must be sewn in the nape of the neck. In suit-type jackets, sewn on the inside pocket. The FTC should be consulted for this information because, if placed incorrectly the label will have to be removed and replaced on each garment at considerable expense to the importer.

4). Basic wash and wear instructions. These must be durable, so as to remain on the garment, even after the garment is cleaned.

Wool
Any product containing woolen fiber, with the exception of items more than 20 years of age, shall be marked as follows:
1). The percentage of total fiber content of the wool exclusive of ornamentation. The total percentage of wool, recycled wool and each fiber other than wool.
2). The maximum percentage of the total weight of the wool product, of any non-fibrous loading, filling or adulterating matter.
3). The name of the manufacturer or importer. A RN# can be used.
4). Wash and wear instructions.

Fur
Any article of wearing apparel, in whole or part of fur requires:
1). Same as #1 of the wool section
2). The names of the animals who produced the fur (as per the Fur Products name guide.)
3). Proof the fur does not contain used or damaged furs

4). Statements as to whether the fur is bleached, dyed, or otherwise colored.
5). Statements declaring whether the fur is in whole or if part paws, tails, bellies and waster products of animal skins were used.
6). Names of all countries of origin of the fur and fur products.

Importers of furs must be certain to consult with the U.S. Fish and Wildlife Service.

Bureau of Radiological Health Phone- (515) 281-3478
For any importation requiring radiation performance standards, such as TV receivers, microwave ovens, x-ray equipment and laser products, imported items must be made available for sampling, but sampling will only be ordered randomly.

FEDERAL COMMUNICATIONS COMMISSION Phone- (888) 225-5322
http://www.fcc.gov/
This commission must review all items relying on receiving or relating to radio waves. Some examples are radios, tape recorders, stereos, televisions, CB radios, and remote telephones. Each item must bear a statement at time of import that the item conforms to FCC standards. CF740 must be filed by the Customs Broker declaring that the radio waves are not harmful or hazardous.

DRUG ENFORCEMENT ADMINISTRATION (DEA) Phone- (202) 305-8500
The DEA monitors all drugs and chemicals to make drugs that are imported into this country. All importers of chemicals are urged to check with the DEA to see if their import might be used in illegal drug production. If the DEA determines that the product is a regulated drug or a chemical that can be used in the production of a regulated or illegal drug, they will require that the importer supply them with all pertinent details concerning where it was manufactured, who is the ultimate consignee in the U.S. and for what purpose it is being imported. The DEA may require that you carefully monitor the disposition of the merchandise, including careful scrutiny of its pickup from the pier/airport and delivery to the consignee. Should any/all of the cargo not arrive at the destination, they are to be informed immediately. As with other government agencies, importers should not be afraid to contact them, in advance of any import, as a discovery process. To avoid or not contact the correct agency is not only a fear but also a serious mistake that could cost an importer thousands of dollars in fines and penalties.

NATIONAL STAMPING ACT (for Gold and Silver)
This act, administered by the Department of Justice, insures the purity and weights of gold and silver. The department sets standards and marking regulations for imports of precious metals, such as 14-carat gold, sterling silver, etc. Failure of gold or silver items to conform to these standards will result in such items becoming a prohibited import.

ENVIRONMENTAL PROTECTION AGENCY (EPA)

Pesticide Regulations
John Larson   303-312-6030   larson.john@epa.gov
Debbie Kovacs   303-312-6020   kovacs.debbie@epa.gov
Mike Rudy   303-312-6785   rudy.mike@epa.gov

Uniform Test Guidelines- http://www.epa.gov/OPPTS_Harmonized/

Pesticide & Insecticide Label Information-
http://www.epa.gov/unix0008/toxics/pests/regs.html#label

To obtain CF3540-1 and information about filing
Contact John Larson (see above)
http://www.epa.gov/unix0008/toxics/pests/import.html

To subscribe to Listserv
http://www.epa.gov/epahome/listserv.htm

Office of Pesticides and Toxic Substances

The EPA monitors any importation of poisons, devices for the manufacture of poisons and pesticides, insecticides, paris greens, lead arsenate's, fungicide, herbicide and rodenticides. On all importation a notice of arrival, EPA Form 3540-1 must be submitted by the Customhouse Broker to the EPA for approval prior to release of the cargo. The EPA reserves the right to sample, test and examine any import for toxicity. The EPA also serves as the agency that would monitor the disposal of any substance deemed a risk to public health or environment. All commercial shipments of toxic articles must obtain an EPA registration number. It is a mandatory requirement for import unless the product:

1. The chemical being imported is used for research and development purposes only.
2. The product is being imported to be reformulated.
3. The product is being temporarily held in the United States or is being transshipped through the United States to an outside destination.
4. The import is returned containers (for refilling or reuse) with only small amounts of pesticides remaining in the container.

DEPARTMENT OF TRANSPORTATION- Phone- (202) 366-4000
Materials Transportation Bureau (Hazardous) Phone- (202) 366-4488

All imports of hazardous substances, including caustic or corrosive material, even those used in household cleaning procedures are controlled and regulated by the above bureau. Transport of the product from the pier or terminal to its ultimate destination must be done with care, and with the truck being marked in a manner prescribed by law that designate that the truck is transporting dangerous goods.

U.S. FISH AND WILDLIFE SERVICE   (800) 358-2104
http://www.fws.gov/r9dia

This agency has jurisdiction over any item that is the product or manufactured from any plant, animal, mammal or fish, including any shellfish that is considered an endangered species.

When importing F&W products, be certain to import them into a port district that has an office of the F&W. Imports into other port districts force the needless transport, in bond, of the product to a port district where there is an office of the F&W. This includes instances where the item is determined not to be a restricted or prohibited item, THE IMPORTER MUST STILL MAKE ENTRY IN A PORT DISTRICT WHERE F&W HAVE AN OFFICE.

Importers of Fish and Wildlife products are required to obtain a permit from the F&W. The cost is $25.00.

In order to research a F&W product, the importer should obtain from the foreign vendor the following information.
1).   Common name of the species
2).   Scientific Name of the species
3).   Country where the Fish &Wildlife product was grown or killed.
       Also, the country where the Fish & Wildlife product was
       manufactured.

Once this information is obtained, seek consultation from the Fish &Wildlife to see if the import is either prohibited, restricted or neither prohibited or restricted. If prohibited, forget about importing it. If restricted, FIND OUT IF A SPECIAL LICENSE OR PERMIT IS REQUIRED FROM THE ORIGINATING COUNTRY. In some cases you may need two licenses, one license (or permit) of legal kill, a second from the country of manufacture. In the case of ivory products, an additional permit is needed showing that the craftsman is licensed to carve ivory, and wastes little if any of the product, as is a requirement of all ivory artisans. Most certificates from foreign governments are called CITIES certificates.

IMPORTATION OF MOTOR VEHICLES

The importer must work with 2 agencies, the DOT and the EPA. U.S. Customs monitors their documents and forms are included and provided on the entry. Bonds are usually obtained through a Customhouse Broker or the authorized converter. While complying vehicles can be imported under a non-secured bond (a fee still applies see page 55). Non-complying vehicles must be imported under 3 bonds, one for Customs + each agency. A security deposit is required, usually 50% of the total bonds. **(example: value of car**

$10,000.00 x 3(bond)= $30,000). A security deposit of $15,000 is required unless the car is handled by a licensed converter.)

National Highway Traffic Safety Administration - Requires form HS-7
U.S. Dept. of Transportation (DOT) Phone (202) 426-1693   (202) 366-5306
(202) 366-5286, (202) 366-6263, (202) 366-0123, (800) 424-9153
http://www.nhtsa.dot.gov/cars/rules/import/
Or e-mail kklass@nhtsa.dot.gov

For vehicles imported for testing purposes
George Entwistle (202) 366-5306

List of U.S. Approved Vehicle Converters (for non-conforming vehicles)
http://www.nhtsa.dot.gov/cars/rules/import/

U.S. Environmental Protection Agency- (EPA)- Requires form 3520-1
Investigation Imports Section (202) 382-2505   (734) 214-4510, fax: (734) 214-4958

When importing any vehicle into the United States one must contact both agencies cited above. Both the EPA & DOT place the same regulations on imported cars that they do for domestic vehicles. Before 1968, there were no restrictions for American or foreign manufactured vehicles. As such, entry procedures are simple for importing a pre-1968 vehicle. Cars manufactured after 1968 are subject to the following regulations based on production year and foreign or domestic manufacturer.

VEHICLE, FOREIGN or DOMESTIC, MANUFACTURED IN ACCORDANCE WITH U.S. STANDARDS

1). Before shipping from the foreign country, obtain a pletezmo certificate, showing that the catalytic converter was changed before being shipped. ESTIMATED COST- $300.00 to $1000.00.
2). If the above certificate cannot be obtained:
   a.) The importer declares to Customs that the vehicle will be converted at an independent, non-government approved conversion facility, THREE, TRIPLE surety bonds (3X the value for DOT, EPA and U.S. Customs) will be a mandatory requirement. For a car with a transaction value of $10,000, three $30,000.00 bonds are required for import.   The total bond value is $90,000. Surety companies usually require a 50% (or more) cash deposit for each bond along with their usual $4.00 per $1000.00 fee.   A $45,000 cash or secured deposit along with the $360.00 fee makes this import cost prohibitive.
   b.) The importer declares to Customs that the vehicle will be converted at an approved government facility, the facility proprietor will clear, bond and deliver the shipment to his workshop, convert and then release to the importer after approval by both agencies.   Estimated cost- $1000-2000.

ANY VEHICLE NOT MANUFACTURED IN ACCORDANCE WITH U.S. STANDARDS

The requirements cited above apply plus the cost of converting the car to U.S. standards. This can range between $5,000.00 and $10,000.00 per vehicle. In addition to previously stated bond requirements.

AN ELECTRIC CAR ON A TEMPORARY BASIS, FOR RACING OR TESTING. Or, a Non-Resident Alien importing a car for less than 1 year for personal use.

Approval from the DOT is usually a simple formality. No EPA review is required except the usual form showing that these items are exempt.

It is the opinion of this author, that unless a vehicle manufactured after 1968 is unique, electrical or solar, has sentimental value, or cannot be obtained in the United States, it is cost prohibitive and risky, and it should not be imported and converted. If the car is stolen, the bonds are forfeited. No converted car can perform as well as a car manufactured in conformity.

Commandant, U.S. Coast Guard **Phone (202) 267-0984   (800) 368-5647 (General)**
In a fashion similar to automobiles, boats must also be imported within the guidelines of the U.S. standards applicable to the year of manufacture. The Coast Guard monitors the safety standards, the EPA (see above) monitors all the pollution requirements and regulations for motor boats.

Patents Trademarks, Tradenames and Copyrights
U.S. Patent and Trademark Office- http://www.uspto.gov/
Phones-   (800) 786-9199 or (703) 308-4357

U.S. Copyright Office- http://lcweb.loc.gov/copyright/
Phone-   (202) 707-3000
Request forms- (202) 707-9100

Importers should NEVER purchase merchandise overseas that is under the protection of a currently held patent, trademark, trade name or copyright unless they obtain authorization from the property holder IN WRITING. Conversely importers who hold patents, trademarks, trade names or copyrights should contact U.S. Customs and file documented evidence to protect their ownership. In addition, an additional copy of the documented proof must be attached to each entry of that product.

If an importer buys a product with trademark, trade name or copyright he must secure a letter from the official holder of the property as evidence of his right to import the product. When buying from a foreign manufacturer of an American patent, trade name or trademark or copyright, the importer must obtain a copy of the manufacturer's authorization BEFORE PURCHASING, and verify it by calling the holder of the patent, trade name, trademark or copyright.

U.S. Customs will seize any cargo suspected of infringing on a patent, trademark, trade name or copyright. Once the cargo is seized, the importer has 30 days to prove, without question, their legal right to import the merchandise. The property holder has an equal amount of time to show if the cargo, indeed, should be confiscated. If it is determined that the property holder's rights were violated, the seized goods are **not subject to return, and are usually destroyed under Customs supervision.** With the loss of the merchandise, this unfortunate importer's troubles are not over, as he is open to prosecution, both civil and criminal for the illegal import.

CHAPTER FOUR

UNDERSTANDING TERMS OF SALE

American importers will never achieve the greatest savings, nor will they achieve optimum control of their purchase, unless they choose to learn and understand international terms of sale. **TERMS OF SALE PROVIDE EXACT INFORMATION** where the sellers' responsibility ceases and the importers' responsibility begins. Without TERMS OF SALE the foreign seller and importer can never be in complete agreement of where the foreign exporters' liability and cost end and where the American importers' risk and expenses begin.

MOST COMMONLY USED TERMS OF SALE

EX-FACTORY - The seller turns the cargo over to the importer at the seller's warehouse or premise. The buyer pays all subsequent charges. (Ex-factory is also known as ex-works, the two terms can be used interchangeably).

FOB (FOREIGN PORT) - The foreign vendor trucks the cargo to the port or terminal where the cargo will be shipped from, pays all trucking, port, Foreign Customs charges (if any), freight forwarding costs, and loading on the aircraft or vessel. The importer pays the international shipping and all charges in the U.S.

CIF (U.S. PORT). The seller pays all charges from his warehouse overseas, to the U.S. port or airport (including insurance). The importer pays for unloading from the vessel or plane, port and terminal charges, Customs formalities and delivery to the ultimate destination.

CIF DDP (DUTY PAID DELIVERED U.S. TOWN) - The seller pays all costs to get the goods from overseas to the ultimate warehouse in the U.S. including U.S. duty and formalities. The importer does nothing but wait for his goods and pay the bill. Buying under these terms is the same as buying cargo from overseas domestically.

Depending on the term of sale, the importer knows what additional charges he must add to the seller's cost.

ITEMIZED COST RESPONSIBILITY
(S- Foreign "seller" or Vendor I- U.S. "Importer)

COSTS	Ex-Works	FOB	CIF	CIFDDP
Seller's invoice	S	S	S	S
Export License	I	S	S	S
Shipment Inspection (overseas)	I	I	I	I
Export Packing	S	S	S	S
Transport to Foreign Port	I	S	S	S
Foreign Port Charges	I	S	S	S
Loading vessel or plane	I	S	S	S
International freight cost	I	I	S	S
U.S. pier/terminal cost	I	I	I	S
U.S. Customs duty/fees	I	I	I	S
U.S. Customs Broker	I	I	I	S
U.S. Loading	I	I	I	S
U.S. Customs Inspection	I	I	I	S
Delivery in U.S.	I	I	I	S
Insurance	I	I	S	S

This chart can leave no doubt in the reader as to the importance of knowing and using terms of sale to their best advantage.

TERMS OF SALE ALWAYS INDICATE A LOCATION
(Some examples)

A manufacturer in Victoria, Spain, offers buyers the option of different prices based on the terms of sale and location.

Wooden office desks- offered at $150.00 each at his factory.
Described as: ***U.S.$150.00 ex-factory Victoria, Spain***

The seller offers the desks at $175.00 each delivered to the port-
Correctly described as ***U.S.$175.00 FOB Bilbao, Spain (port)***

The seller offers the desks at $225.00 each delivered to the U.S. port including the all-risk marine insurance.
Completely shown as: ***U.S.$225.00 CIF Port of New York***
The seller offers the desks at $300.00 each, delivered duty paid to the importers warehouse. The seller is responsible for all costs, the buyer in the U.S. is accepting imported goods on a domestic basis. The buyer is no longer the importer. The seller, or his agent, must be the importer. The correct way to describe the purchase price is:

Using complete terms of sale leaves no doubt as to the liability, risk and expenses of both the buyer and the seller.

Recommendations of which terms of sale to use, and when!

1. Importers buying small or sample shipments should try to push the seller to offer a price of either CIF delivered, or CIF delivered duty paid. The seller often ships these small orders to many prospective buyers in the United States at the same time, reducing the overall cost.

"COMMON SENSE EXAMPLE- EGGS ARE SOLD BY THE DOZEN, 1 &1/2 Dozen, Case, Gross, etc. To pack, ship and sell one or two eggs would wind up with a cost very close to the dozen. There is a minimum cost for labor, trucking, handling and profit. The same concept carries through to international shipping. Ocean freight cargoes usually ship as a minimum of 1 cubic meter or metric ton. To ship a tenth or quarter of a ton or cubic meter costs the same as the entire ton or meter. If an insurer charges 1% to insure cargo- (example $10,000.00 shipment - insurance cost = $100.00) what about a $500.00 shipment? $5.00 is not enough to cut a policy, so most insurance companies have minimum policy of about $50.00.

When offered a "reasonable" CIF cost by the seller for sample or small shipments save the time and trouble of useless sourcing, using the seller's price, as long as it seems reasonable. Consider mail for samples when the items are small enough and you can wait a few weeks for them.

2. Regular and substantial orders: Once a decision is made to issue a purchase order and commence buying merchandise for inventory (drop shipments or in quantity), or as a commercial shipment for any purpose, an importer must look into the options of purchasing goods under the terms that are favorable to his expenses and his control of the shipment. Perhaps the greatest avenue for reducing landed cost is through cutting shipping costs. On CIF, Delivered and Duty paid shipments, the seller is providing all services to get the cargo either to the United States or to your door, in addition to the cost of the merchandise. As in any business, this service is not provided free of charge. The vendor often will work with his own freight forwarder, and mark up the cost offered from his forwarder as an additional way of making a profit.

When foreign cargo is purchased under FOB or ex-factory terms, the importer must nominate the freight forwarder, and indicate to his foreign vendor whom to contact to ship the cargo. This nomination should be stipulated by the importer on both the purchase order and letter of credit. Please refer to (page 38-39).

If a vendor offers only a CIF price and refuses to offer an FOB or EX-FACTORY cost, the importer is still left with some options:

a). Buy at the CIF cost, but realize that you probably are paying a lot more to get the goods than you should.

b). By using a representative or buying agent in the exporting country, an importer can see if the vendor will sell the same item domestically on an ex-factory basis (ex-works). If the importer currently works with an American freight forwarder, his agent in that country might be able to obtain the information for the importer.

c). Push the vendor again. The importer can site that he is consolidating goods overseas (which is combining goods from more than one vendor together in order to save on freight rates and clearance costs). The importer can advise the vendor, that, if forced to buy under CIF terms, they need a complete breakdown as to all auxiliary charges (international shipping, destination charges, insurance, etc.) in an effort to compare these rates with the rates they pay to their current consolidator. After all, the importer does not want to have to pay higher shipping costs than he has to. In many instances, the foreign seller will try his best to keep the sales at CIF, but relent to the buyer when it means losing a sale. It often helps for the importer to have two or more sources for the same product, and to play one off against the other. If a vendor's product is unique and has no competition he can afford to keep his prices high and dictate the terms of sale to be CIF. Find another vendor of similar products and force the seller to remain competitive. ALL IMPORTERS SHOULD HAVE, WHENEVER POSSIBLE MORE THAN ONE VENDOR TO BUY CARGO FROM.

CHAPTER FIVE

LANDED COST

Landed cost is the total cost of getting the merchandise to its destination in these United States plus the value of the goods. All import companies calculate a landed cost so that they do not purchase a foreign product and go through the trouble of importing it only to discover that they have spent more money than they can sell it for. It is very important to know TERMS OF SALE (see Chapter #3) in order to calculate an accurate landed cost. The following list details all possible costs, but be careful to only include them in your calculations when they are not already paid for by the seller.

OVERSEAS FORMALITIES
Foreign trucking, foreign pier and terminal charges, foreign duty, customs fees, and freight forwarding fees.

The importer should only be concerned with these fees when buying under terms of sale EX-WORKS. In all other instances these charges are paid for by the seller and included in the price. When buying under ex-works terms of sale, the importer should obtain a quote for additional charges that includes all shipping costs from FACTORY (overseas) to WAREHOUSE or CUSTOMER (in the U.S.) (See page 40), from a freight forwarder who has an office in the United States.

INTERNATIONAL FREIGHT COSTS
Ocean freight and air freight, from Port to Port or Airport to Airport
When buying under CIF terms the seller pays these costs and the importer knows they are included in the cost of the merchandise. When buying FOB or ex-works, the importer should get costs from freight forwarders with offices in the U.S. and designate the forwarders – foreign counterpart (in the country of export), to the seller on the purchase order and the Letter of Credit, if issued.

U.S. PORT AND TERMINAL COSTS
Destination Delivery Charges (DDC), Terminal Handling Charges (THC), Bunker and Fuel Surcharge (BAF), Currency Adjustment Factor (CAF).

> *For CIF DELIVERED and CIF DUTY PAID DELIVERED*
> The seller pays for these charges, and they are included in the cost that the importer pays for the merchandise.

For CIF purchases
The importer must PAY THESE PORT AND TERMINAL COSTS. These are often "hidden" from the importer, who becomes surprised as he failed to realize that he would be responsible for them. The costs can be almost half as high as the freight cost, as illustrated by the following examples-

COMMON "COLLECT" DESTINATION CHARGES ON FREIGHT PREPAID SHIPMENTS

From	Less than container	20' container	40' container
Europe	$35.00 per w/m*	$500.00	$600.00
Far East	$35.00 per w/m*	$535.00	$1070.00

These costs are approximate, and can be more or less in certain instances. W/M refers to Weight/Measure (see page 42). The point is, be aware these exist!

DEFINITIONS:
Carriers, Forwarders and Consolidators-

Carriers are the companies that actually own the vessels and airplanes that transport cargo (airlines and steamship companies). Freight forwarders (also usually consolidators) have contracts with the carriers that offer them a substantial discount in return for shipping a large amount of freight, usually over a one year period. If importers try to ship a small amount of cargo directly with the carrier, they must pay the tariff rate, which can sometimes more than double the rate that a freight forwarder is paying. Freight forwarders pass on part of the savings that they get to the importer, as well as furnishing them with many additional services, such as regular communication and tracking, that a carrier cannot. A consolidator groups together more than one foreign vendors cargo, or, more than one importer's cargo and combines it in a container. The consolidator has an excellent rate for shipping a full container and, while still making a profit, offering a great savings to the importer. Most forwarders are consolidators.

LOCATE AND WORK WITH A FREIGHT FORWARDER
In order to obtain the best combination of service and price for your import shipments, it is advisable to always research the additional charges associated with shipping the merchandise to their ultimate destination in the United States. Any importer should actively seek and work with a freight forwarder in the United States who either has an office or a partner in the country of manufacture overseas. A freight forwarder can be located through referrals, embassies, U.S. trade associations, Port Authorities in U.S. ports, and phone directories. Thousands of international freight forwarders operate in the United States. An importer should call or fax numerous freight forwarders in order to

obtain quotes for the cost of shipping the cargo, as well as what other kinds of services they offer. Be sure to research the transit time as well. A rate to ship goods may be excellent, but a 60-day transit time (instead of a 25-30 day one) reveals why the cost is so low.

A lot can be determined about forwarders, as in any other business, by the initial contact. There is no doubt in this writer's mind, that if any business has trouble receiving a phone call or fax asking for rates, or takes too long to responding to the request, this is a very good indication that the company either has either too much work or is incompetent. Neither option seems very pleasant to an importer who needs his forwarder to communicate with him on a regular basis.

Once a few of your initial contacts seem to be able and willing to offer a quote, and service the intended area of transit, the following REQUEST FOR A RATE QUOTE should be faxed to them all:

SEE NEXT PAGE

EXAMPLE OF FAXED RATE REQUEST FORM

FROM: ANY U.S. IMPORTER, CO. INC.
123 Pennsylvania Avenue Any town, USA

TO: To- ABC FORWARDING   FAX#-

RE- Request for a rate quote-
Commodity _____ Pallets? _____ Cartons _____
Weight _____ Size of package(s) LxWxH _____

Please advise my costs for the following shipment
Air cost _____   Ocean Cost _____   Both _____
From __(factory location)   To ___(ultimate destination)

Terms of sale   Ex-works _____   FOB _____   CIF _____
Cost (of cargo) _____   Insurance needed ____

Special shipping arrangements FCL only _____
Flatbed needed _____ Refrigerated _____ Hazardous ___
Other _____
_____

Your overnight reply is valued- Be sure to include inclusive cost-
Is the DDC, THC, BAF and CAF CY and all costs included?
Can you also clear Customs, at what cost? _____
Do you charge a transfer fee? _____
What is the frequency of sailings/flights ? _____
What is the transit time? _____
How long is this rate valid for? _____

Always check with more than one forwarder. Faxing a half dozen or more companies using a computer or word processor is not that difficult or time consuming. Don't just let the overseas seller quote you one CIF or CIFDDP price and blindly accept it, check out the alternatives. Why pay more than you have to? The goal is to get the lowest possible landed cost to be competitive, so:

1. Get a list of U.S. freight forwarders who call on the country of exportation.
2. Fax rate quote requests to all of them, and compare costs and services.

Benefits to an Importer to Designate the Freight Forwarder

1. The importer can consult with a company or person familiar with international shipping. As a regular client the importer can rely upon the forwarder for information on their shipment and quotes for different services.
2. Should an importer need to have the goods checked for quality control, the freight forwarder's counterpart in the country of export can arrange this.
3. The forwarder can keep track of your shipment, letting you know when it is shipped or arriving. The importer is no longer at the mercy of the shipper and the shipper's agent.
4. The importer can lock in a shipping cost that he can rely upon for an accurate landed cost, often up to a year.
5. The importer can be advised of transit schedules and frequency of sailings or flights with the complete inclusive rate. Once this information is evaluated, the forwarder is advised IN WRITING BY FAX or e-mail of how to ship the merchandise.
6. The importer can import cargo without his identity becoming public domain. When importing directly with a carrier, the information on a bill of lading is freely circulated. However, when importing with a forwarder, the forwarder's particulars are revealed to the public records, camouflaging the importer.

KNOW THE PACKAGE SIZE AND WEIGHT

At the same time the seller is offering a cost for his product, he also should be advising you of the weight and size of the items being shipped. If it is uniform packing, then each carton should be the same size and weight. If different, the supplier should be able to furnish you with a breakdown of the weight of each carton and its dimensions. It is important to have a basic knowledge of the metric system. In most cases, cargo shipped via vessel is shipped at a cost based on either the weight or the volume, whichever is greater.

If goods were only shipped by volume, then a person shipping feathers would be paying too much, a person shipping lead weights too little. If they were shipped based on weights, the reverse would apply. So the method described below has been developed to evenly access the costs of shipping goods by ocean.

Working with Ocean Freight Rates

Ocean freight cargo rates are currently calculated by the greater of:

METRIC TON (1000 kgs) or CUBIC METER (1 cbm)
(W/M - weight measure)   (M/T - CBM)

When less than a m/t or cbm is shipped, the carrier/forwarder usually charges for one m/ton or one cbm rate.

Some carriers (usually ones who serve the Caribbean) ship freight on a ratio of 1000 pounds or 40 cubic feet. Other carriers may increase the rate for less than container loads (lcl), when the cargo is discharged on either coast, then trucked overland to an inland destination, due to the cost of domestic trucking. In such cases it is not uncommon for a rate structure to be based on a conversion of 330kgs = 1 cubic meter.

STANDARD CONVERSIONS-   2.2046 pounds = 1 kilo
                              35.28 cubic feet = 1 cubic meter

Example of freight rates--
    $90.00 per w/m. (weight/measure). (metric ton or cubic meter)
    To ship .5 (half a meter) cost = $90.00
    To ship 1 meter = $90.00
    To ship 5 meters and 3000 kilos = 5cbm = $450.00
    If cargo was 5 meters and 6000 kilos = 6m/t = $540.00

Most cargo is shipped based on CUBIC METER unless it is extremely heavy. A large crate of books, equal to a cubic meter, would weigh about 500 kilos, and still ship by Cubic Meter, not Metric Ton.

Metals and machinery, on the other hand, are heavy enough to have the rates based on the weight, and have a ratio of greater than 1 metric ton per cubic meter. It is always important to get an accurate size of the packing from the shipper, so that the cost for shipping can be calculated in advance of placing the purchase order.

INCLUSIVE FREIGHT RATE

All forwarders should be encouraged to quote an inclusive freight rate whenever possible. The following costs can be assessed by forwarders, separately from the freight cost, or combined with it for a total inclusive cost. International freight cost, technically can be viewed as just the cost from the foreign port to U.S. Port. Getting the cargo on and off the vessel, port costs, fuel and currency adjustment costs can all be added on, UNLESS IT IS AGREED AHEAD OF TIME THAT THEY ARE INCLUDED IN THE BASE OCEAN FREIGHT COSTS.

DDC-	*(Destination Delivery Charge)*	*For pier charges in U.S.*
THC-	*(Terminal Handling Charge)*	*Similar to DDC*
CAF-	*(Currency Adjustment Factor)*	*Surcharge in percentage*
BAF-	*(Bunker And Fuel Surcharge)*	*Percentage added to base*

When a forwarder does not wish to quote an all inclusive rate, get a detailed breakdown of all additional charges.

Advantage to shipping "Full Containers"

Most cargo, when not overweight or oversized, is shipped in standard containers. The ocean carriers (who own or lease the containers) provide them, including their usage as part of the freight cost. Each carrier will have a standard rate tariff, which they use to calculate the freight cost based on the commodity and point of origin and destination. However, shippers and consignees (exporters, importers and forwarders) can negotiate contracts with the carriers agreeing to ship a minimum amount of containers (usually from 100 to 1000s) and in doing so obtain a significant price discount from the tariff rate, OFTEN AS HIGH AS A 50% discount. It is not unusual for large traders and exporters to ship as many as 10,000 containers per year! The carrier, in agreeing to the lower rate, enforces a penalty for contract holders who fail to meet their commitment, usually hundreds of dollars for each container not shipped.

It makes little or no sense for exporters and importers to contact carriers to get shipping rates, unless they are certain to ship at least 100 containers via that shipping line. However, the contract rate to ship 100 containers is still considerably higher than the multi-thousand contract rate secured by large forwarders, who still can offer a better rate to the importer.

Forwarders pass part of the savings on to the importer, often a large portion, as many other forwarders are scrambling for the same business. Other reasons to employ a freight forwarder are detailed on page 47.

STANDARD CONTAINER SIZES

It is of great advantage to ship cargo as an full container. When an importer buys enough cargo to ship as a full container, the container is brought to the vendor, cargo loaded and the door sealed. Unless Customs (in the exporting or importing country) is intending to examine the cargo, the door is not reopened until it arrives at the ultimate destination in the United States. It is less expensive to ship a full container than less than container. Cargo is loaded and packed by the shipper, allowing him to safeguard the contents. It will not be reloaded, shifted or transferred again unless a Customs exam is required.

The following are the standard sizes of containers. In addition to the size consideration, importers should keep in mind the maximum allowable weight. After the container is pulled from the pier the weight cannot exceed the maximum weight allowed on highways in that area.

Prices to ship a container are usually based on a flat price. This price should be an all inclusive price, similar to the ones illustrated on page 45.

Maximum weight can vary by port of import, the weight stated below is an average for the United States.

20'- 20'x8'x8' (L x W x H). Maximum weight allowed is 36,000 pounds
    Actual interior space- 1280 cubic feet- Usable space-1000 cft.

40'- 40'x 8'x 8' (L x W x H). Maximum weight allowed is 44,000 pounds
    Actual interior space 2560 cubic feet. Usable space- 2000 cft

45'- 45'x 8'x 8' (L x W x H). Maximum weight allowed is 44,000 pounds
    Actual interior space- 2880 cubic feet Usable space- 2300 cft

40'HQ 40'x 8' x 9'6" Maximum weight allowed is 44,000 pounds
    Actual interior space- 3040 cubic feet Usable space- 2600 cft.

Usable cubic feet is subject to change. A shipment of heavy machines may only take up half the space in a container, but odd sizes will prohibit any additional cargo from being put into the container. If cargo is uniformly packed the usable space can almost be the actual space, but if it is floor loaded the importer must consider the extra time and expense to have the goods hand-loaded. Palletized cargo is safer to ship, as it is harder to shift during the ocean voyage. Pallets are usually 40" x 48", letting 2 rows of 5 pallets in a 20' container (10 pallets). If stackable, 20 pallets.   For a 40' container 20 pallets, 40 pallets if stackable. For a 45' container- 22 pallets, 44, if stackable.

Weights in a conventional container vary from port district to port district. Regulations in Chicago have a lower maximum cargo weight, while in Dallas, the weight is higher. Local port districts should be contacted when trying to discover the legal maximum weight of a container.

For overweight containers, special equipment does exist, but the special chassis must be rented or obtained at the destination. The steamship line often provides these special chassis, sometimes they can be provided by the trucker who picks up the cargo. Average additional cost for this special equipment is $200.00 per unit.   Examples of special equipment are:

Slider chassis The chassis (wheeled base of a container), slides out to distribute the weight more evenly. You can add about another 5,000 pounds when using a slider chassis.

Tri-axle chassis Three sets of wheels are now under the container, thus distributing the weight more evenly. Add up to 7,000 pounds when using a tri-axle chassis.

Multi-axled chassis Cargo weighing upwards of 100,000 pounds can be imported and successfully trucked from the pier. Specialized cartsman have chassis with up to 12 sets of wheels, allowing for the weight to be distributed over the many axles. The cost can increase dramatically, however, when shipping very heavy machinery or rock products, there are really no other options.

Open top containers For cargo that must be lowered by crane.
Flat rack containers For over wide cargo.
Refrigerated (reefer containers) Temperature control and refrigerated cargo.

Break Bulk Cargo
When cargo cannot fit into a conventional container, or onto specialized equipment, it is shipped in the hold of a vessel, or if liquid, in large tanks or holds, known as "Break Bulk" cargo. Container carriers generally do not ship break bulk cargo. Freight rates for shipping break bulk cargo usually remains the same for dry cargo, based on cubic meter or metric ton or, if liquid, on the metric equivalent for fluids. However, bulk loading and unloading is far more complicated and expensive than container freight. Cost for loading, time vessel is kept in port, as well as at destination also have to be known before estimating any costs. Shipping bulk and charter vessels is a science unto itself and any importer is urged to contact a forwarder experienced in that field..

Working with Air Freight Rates
Air shipments are costed based on a comparison of the weight and measure, but to a much stricter standard. A formula to use is as follows:

CUBIC FEET x 10.4 = DIMENSIONAL WEIGHT

EXAMPLE 10 bales of fabric - 600 pounds 200 cubic feet
Multiply the total cubic feet x 10.4-
200 x 10.4 = 2,080 dimensional weight
As the 2,080 dimensional weight is higher, the rate for shipment is charged based on the dimensional weight, not the actual weight.

EXAMPLE- 5 machines   total- 2000 pounds - 100 cubic feet
100 x 10.4= 1,040 dimensional weight
As the actual weight is higher, the freight rate is based on 2,000 pounds.

Any air shipment must be checked to see if it will be shipped under actual weight or dimensional weight.

Importers should be forewarned that freight rates are significantly higher during December with the onrush of passengers on planes. As a result there is less room for cargo, which is then shipped on cargo and charter planes. The backlog can delay airfreight for up to 2 weeks, unless the importer is willing to pay top dollar to ship the cargo.

As with ocean containers, airlines and air consolidators (freight forwarders), have mini-containers which are unloaded and de-vanned at outside warehouses, brought to the plane and then shipped. While these mini-containers often offer better freight rates, an additional cost to bring them to the terminal often offsets the savings.

Air freight is generally offered in size breakdowns, such as

Minimum to 45 kgs	45-100 kgs	100-200 kgs
200-500 kgs	500- 1,000 kgs	over 1,000 kgs

SPOT RATES
Usually freight rates offered by freight forwarders are substantially lower than shipping with an airline directly (often as much as half the cost or more!). Spot rates are offered for shipments higher 1000 kilos. These special rates offer a tremendous savings from normal rates because of the large amount of the freight. Spot rates are only offered by carriers to forwarders, not to individuals or companies. It is always in the importer's best interest to get rates from more than one forwarder, as some specialize in a specific global area. Once an importer decides to use a specific forwarder always call in advance to "book" (reserve) space for shipment to avoid lengthy delays.

Conventional aircraft used to carry passengers also carry commercial shipments in their hold when there is room. There are limitations as to the size of the packages that can be shipped on passenger airlines. Air charters and cargo planes have an upper and lower deck, to accommodate larger shipments and planes are available that can ship tanks and even small buildings!

Summary of Ocean freight and Air freight rates
When requesting freight rates, ALWAYS be sure to get the rate to as close to the ultimate destination as possible. Most major cities in the U.S. are indeed U.S. Customs points of entry for both air and ocean cargo. Air cargo can be shipped by air to an international airport, then shipped "in bond" via plane or truck to any major inland point. Ocean shipments certainly arrive at ports on the coasts. However full containers are sent by rail or truck to inland points throughout this country.

The largest use of this system is called "mini-land bridge". Most of the tremendous volume of cargo from the far east arrives on the West Coast and then entire trains of containers are sent via rail to almost every major city in the mid-west and east coast. This method of shipping is about 1-2 weeks faster than the all-water route via the Panama

Canal. It is also more expensive. All consolidators ship LCL cargo from the Far East via mini-land bridge.

TRANSIT TIMES - OCEAN CARGOES-

	From Far East	From Europe
To East Coast Via Water	28-50 days	7-15 days
To East Coast via Mini-Land bridge	16-35 days	-------------
To-West Coast via Water	10-22 days	25-35 days
To-West Coast via (East coast rail)	-------------	18-25 days

U.S. Customs allows the in-bond movement of freight from the actual ports of entry of the vessels to inland points via rail and truck. **IT IS ALWAYS BETTER TO TRANSPORT CARGO TO A LOCATION AS CLOSE TO THE ULTIMATE DESTINATION AS POSSIBLE. SECURE RATE QUOTES BASED ON THESE DESTINATIONS. THEY ARE FAR BETTER THAN TRYING TO TRANSPORT THE CARGO THERE AFTER IMPORTING IT TO A PORT OR LOCATION A GREAT DISTANCE AWAY.** This applies to CIF shipments as well as FOB. If you are buying CIF, be sure to have the shipper quote you a rate to the closest Customs point of entry. For example, if an importer is shipping to Columbus, Ohio, (or vicinity) get a rate from the FOB (foreign port) to Columbus, Ohio, from the freight forwarder. If an importer is shipping to the Denver, Colorado, vicinity, he MUST secure a rate to Denver, not to just the port of arrival. This is a key point to achieving the best rates and transit times possible.

THE ADVANTAGE OF CENTRAL COORDINATION
When an importer makes an FOB or ex-works purchase, he must work with the following services to get the cargo to its destination:

    a). The freight forwarder who ships from overseas to the U.S.
    b). The Customhouse Broker who clears the cargo in the U.S.
    c). The trucker who transports the cargo from pier or airport.

A freight forwarder can be asked for a rate for a "through delivery," arranging transport from FOB foreign port, all dock formalities and have the cargo trucked to the ultimate destination. In many instances the forwarder is also a Customhouse Broker and can arrange clearance. This can be of the utmost advantage to the importer, since:

1). By using only one import service agent, the importer only has to make ONE call to find out the status of his shipment, instead of three.
2). By allowing one party to handle all three services, it is easy to request a faxed, or e-mailed tracking report, updating the status of the shipment.

3). If something goes wrong, there is only one party who could be responsible. Without doubt, when using three different parties (a forwarder, broker and trucker), each will try to place liability on the other for any mishap, error or omission.

4). The forwarder must send paperwork to the broker. The broker in turn must send documents to the trucker as well as payment and bill of lading to the forwarder. The result when using three separate services can be upwards of a two-day delay in processing documents. This format is obviously not the most efficient use of time. Needless to say, each vendor must make a profit, so use of one vendor is often cost effective as well.

5). The importer cannot be charged a transfer fee (the charge for the forwarder turning over documents to the broker, usually between $35 and $60) to get the documents from the forwarder to the broker. He also cannot be charged a messenger fee to get the delivery order to the trucking company. Each task is considered the forwarder's own, inherent in-house responsibility when handling all three above activities.

On CIF Purchases- THE IMPORTER STILL PAYS!
The importer is still responsible to pay all destination charges such as DDC or THC. This cost can be almost as expensive as the prepaid freight. Currently the following charges are destination fees, which the importer must pay when buying CIF.

From	To	LCL	20'container	40'container
Far East (as high as)	East Coast	$35.00*	$535.00**	$1070.00**
Europe (as high as)	East Coast	$35.00*	$500.00**	$600.00**

For less than container load $35.00 per revenue ton (1 cbm or 1 metric ton).
**For full container loads a flat fee, as above, applies.*

Always be sure to add these charges into your cost when buying CIF and be prepared to pay these charges when the cargo arrives. Many importers have failed to calculate this charge to their landed cost when buying CIF.

When buying ex-works or FOB
Always try to get an inclusive charge from the freight forwarder. On ocean shipments, ask that the quote include DDC, THC, BAF and CAF. On air shipments be certain that terminal and transfer charges are also included, as some air forwarders charge the importer for switching the cargo to their warehouse. If the forwarder does not include the charge, be sure they tell you that the charge is not accessed!

Loading and document fees at the terminal or port
After cargo arrives at the port, terminal or warehouse, the importer is assessed for loading the cargo onto the truck that picks up the cargo (for less than container load only), and a document fee for both full and loose containers. The following rates, applicable to the Port of New York, are probably the highest in the country.

Loading onto Truck	$3.45 per hundred pounds $38. minimum
Documentation fee	$30.00
Total minimum charge	$68.00 paid at time of pick up

Consider that to truck 20,000 pounds (for a local delivery) can cost, for example $1.20 per hundred weight (cwt). Loading costs would be **ALMOST THREE TIMES THE COST OF THE DELIVERY!**

When feasible cargo should be loaded on pallets overseas. This eases the material handling at the warehouse of destination. However, be sure to alert the foreign vendor to **USE WOOD FREE FROM BARK AND PESTS, AS WELL AS HEAT TREATED**. A statement to this effect should be placed on both the commercial invoice and bill of lading. If necessary, the wood should be fumigated and an appropriate fumigation certificate issued. *

FUMIGATION PLUS CERTIFICATION FOR ANY WOOD CRATING OR PALLETS IS NOW MANDATORY FOR SHIPMENTS FROM CHINA!

Trucking from the ports or airport to ultimate destination
Some truckers specialize in shipping imported freight, which is a different science than domestic freight. Domestic freight charges are based on a class (each different type of merchandise has a different class), and a weight breakdown between points (zip code to zip code). Knowing the weight and size of any shipment, or if it is a full container will enable the importer to get rate quotes and see who can move the cargo most efficiently and most economically. Imported freight charges are usually based on a flat rate from port or air terminal to destination. Any usual waiting time at the place of pickup is included in the flat rate. Class rates are seldom used, unless the freight cannot be shipped by conventional means, for example, hazardous or over gauge freight.

Full Containers-
Full containers rates are charged a rate based on the mileage from the port to ultimate destination, as well as the mileage to return the container to the port or railhead.

Some savings can be achieved by finding out if the container can be returned to a different location, perhaps closer to the delivery address. Also, sometimes one trucker will handle most of the work for a particular steamship company or forwarder, and be able to offer a rate a lot less than normally can be obtained.

For deliveries that are hundreds of miles from origin, a savings can often be achieved if a local trucking company picks up the cargo, brings it to his or a local warehouse and has the cargo "swung" to an over-the-road carrier. This frees up the steamship line's equipment for a local return, and the cargo can be delivered on a one-way basis to its destination.

Usually, trucking companies give the warehouse at destination two free hours to unload the container after which they charge a fee of about $40 per hour for waiting time. The driver is responsible for helping to move the cargo to the back of the truck, whenever possible, except when a forklift is the only means to move heavy freight, be they on pallets or not. Containers can also be dropped at their destination, whereby the tractor detaches itself from the trailer and leaves the container to be unloaded overnight or over a weekend. This method is especially useful when importing two or more containers, as the trucking company brings one loaded container, drops it and picks up the empty one. When multiple containers do not exist, the trucking company will charge between 50-100% of the original quote to go back and pick up the empty.

Less than a container load- loose freight-
Some truck men specialize in freight to and from the piers, warehouses and terminals. Often they serve as an intermediate, picking up from the pier and then delivering to the over-the-road trucker. Every port, ramp or airport must have many, trucking companies who can be checked for rates. Often, it is easier to have the broker or forwarder offer rates, as they are aware of reliable, as well as economical pier trucking company. There is no doubt that they broker and forwarder are making a commission on this trucking. But if the rate and service are better than an importer can obtain for themselves, it must be expected and not considered unreasonable. As such, it is considered disreputable for the importer to contact the trucker assigned by the broker/forwarder and try to deal directly with them. Trucking companies usually charge by the hundred weight with a minimum or maximum. Unless same-day delivery is specified, delivery usually refers to pick up one day and delivery the next.

U.S. Customs duties and fees-

U.S. Customs assesses duties based on the tariff rate applicable to any given product. These rates are listed in the Harmonized Tariff of the United States, which are updated each year. There are over 30,000 tariff items, in a book that is over 4 inches thick. The tariff is broken down into 100 chapters, by subject, then into hundreds of individual categories, by item or type. Each item has three different duty rates, based on what country the item imported is grown, manufactured or produced. Every country in the world fits into at least one of these columns unless a country has banned trade status with the U.S. (such as Cuba). These countries having different duty rates are grouped in columns, Columns 1, 2 and a Special column.

a). Column 1 (Most favored nations status)
Most countries in the world have duties rates applicable to this column, except for PROHIBITED COUNTRIES such as CUBA, LIBYA, IRAQ, IRAN, etc. and countries denied most favored nation status (Duty shown

in Column 2). Many favored nations are eligible for preferential treatment under the "SPECIAL" column for MANY BUT NOT ALL items.

b). Column 2 (Countries not granted favored nation status)
These rates were first imposed in 1930. Being excessively high, as a protectionist cure to the Great Depression (1929-1939), they can range up to 100% of the entered value. Column 2 countries are- LAOS, CAMBODIA, CUBA, AFGHANISTAN, and NORTH KOREA.

c) Special rates of duty (Free and Reduced duty rates).
The following programs exists that lower or eliminate the duty rates for many (but not all) products from certain nations, or groups of nations.

GSP- General System of Preferences for Underdeveloped Countries. (Most of Eastern Europe, near east, Africa, South America)
CBI- Caribbean Basin Initiative. Free status to almost all of the Caribbean
Israeli-U.S. Trade Agreement-
North American- (Canada and Mexico)

Importers can discover duty rates either from the Harmonized Code, calling U.S. Customs (as detailed on page 12 and also U.S. Customs internet page 15. For guaranteed duty rates, file for a binding ruling as shown on page 16.

Customs fees

U.S. Customs collects duties to add to the Treasury of the United States. It collects user fees to pay for its own budget, and harbor fees to raise funds for the Army Corps of Engineers to dredge the harbors of sludge and waste so large container ships can enter each port. The fees collected are

User fee-   .21%- $2.10 per $1000.00 value
                   $25.00 minimum $485.00 maximum
                   Informal entries user fee - usually $2.00

Harbor fee-   .125% $1.25 per $1000.00 value
                   Harbor fee has no minimum or maximum

Customs fees are collected at time of entry along with the Duty.

TRANSACTION VALUE - CUSTOMS METHOD FOR VALUATION

U.S. Customs uses a formula known as transaction value to determine what will be the entered value of merchandise arriving in these United States. The reader may question, "why not just use the invoice value?" Or conversely, why not use a price appraised by Customs? Either way would hinder fair trade as well as offer an unreliable method of determining the value, in advance, for each and every import. Examples of the unfairness of a uniform invoice value being used to determine dutiable value are as follows:

An importer pays $50.00 ex-works Dublin for a desk in Ireland

Another pays $75.00 CIF duty paid delivered Brooklyn

If Customs charges 3% duty for the desk the first importer would have to pay $1.50 duty per desk on an ex-works purchase and the second importer would pay $2.25 duty per desk on a CIF DPD purchase? Would that be fair?

No, it wouldn't be fair. To "level the playing field" for all importers U.S. Customs accesses duty, usually on the value, via an organized system known as *"Transaction Value."*

INVOICE VALUE
The price stated on the commercial invoice of the foreign seller. The price should also indicate TERMS OF SALE and LOCATION. This value should be the cost actually paid by the importer for the merchandise, and can be substantiated with letter of credit, banking or other documentation, if needed.

ENTERED VALUE
The entered value is determined by correctly using the regulations of transaction value, and is based on the invoice value. Depending what costs are, or are not, included in the invoice value, plus other payments that might have been made related to the same transaction, costs are added or deducted from the invoice value to obtain the entered value. The entered value, rounded to the nearest dollar is, the amount upon which the importer pays U.S. Customs duties and fees.

Transaction value was instituted as a uniform means of valuation, so that all importers, whether they were buying ex-works, FOB,. CIF or CIF Duty Paid Delivered were subject to the same basis of value appraisement. Taking the actual purchase price reflected on the commercial invoice as its basis, it specifies certain auxiliary charges to be dutiable or non-dutiable IF included or NOT included in the purchase price.

BASIC RULES FOR TRANSACTION VALUE (abridged)

First, Is the Purchase Price (invoice value) Legitimate?
Probably over 99% of all entries use TRANSACTION value as the means of appraisement and valuation. TRANSACTION VALUE cannot be used in certain situations where the value stated on the invoice is not accurate, tainted, misleading or incorrect. Examples of when transaction value is not correct are:

1. Restriction
The seller imposes a restriction on the buyer's disposition of the merchandise and, as such, the value is not what would be normally charged if the restriction didn't exist.

2. Condition of sale
The buyer agrees to purchase other goods, or perform other services for the seller so as to artificially inflate or deflate the value shown on the invoice.

3. Proceeds
If part of the proceeds accrue to the seller as a prearranged agreement for purchase, then the original purchase price cannot be accurate.

4. Relationship
The buyer and seller are related, such as direct family relation (brother, sister, mother, etc.), partners in business (owning 5% or more of the other party's business), employer/employee or officers in each other's company.

The above four reasons DO NOT AUTOMATICALLY eliminate transaction value as a means of appraisement, but subject the entry to a strict analysis as to whether the price shown on the invoice is indeed unaffected by any or all of the reasons stated. If unaffected then transaction value can be used.

ADDITIONS TO TRANSACTION VALUE
If any of the following additional charges exist, but are not included in the invoice price, they must be added to the invoice price and be considered part of the entry value. They are:

a. Packing
If packing is not included in the invoice price than it must be added as a dutiable value.

b. Selling commission
If the buyer must pay a selling commission to a third party who arranged the sale on behalf of the seller, then this commission or cost is dutiable, and should be added to the invoice cost.

c. Assists
An assist is any of the following items that the buyer will provide to the seller, at free or reduced cost for use in the production or sale of the merchandise to the United States:

1. Materials, components or any item incorporated in the sale item.
2. Tools, dies or molds used in production.
3. Items consumed in production such as fuel.
4. Engineering, blueprints, artwork, design work that is undertaken "outside of the U.S."

Any assist must be added to the invoice value ALONG WITH THE COST OF GETTING THE ASSIST TO THE SELLER. THESE COSTS ARE DUTIABLE!

d. Royalty or License fee

e. Proceeds
Any proceed or charge payable back to the seller is dutiable, and added to the invoice value.

DEDUCTIONS FROM TRANSACTION VALUE
The following list of items, IF included in the cost of the merchandise is considered NON-DUTIABLE and can be deducted at time of entry from the transaction value for entry purposes. Importers are cautioned that for an ex-works transaction, the insurance and international freight are NEVER deductible, as they are paid separately and in no way part of the commercial invoice.

a. International Freight
On any CIF (CIFDP, CIFDPD) transaction, the international freight is non-dutiable. When shipping from a landlocked country, the cost from the border of the exporting country to the port or airport of departure is also non-dutiable when included in the cost.

b. Buying commission
If the invoice cost includes any commission paid to an agent of the importer, then that commission is non-dutiable and can be deducted from the dutiable cost.

c. Insurance
On any CIF transaction, the insurance cost is non-dutiable and can be deducted from the entered value.

d. Duty
On any CIF DP (duty paid) transaction, the duty and any Customhouse Brokerage fee can be deducted to create the entered value.

e. Foreign inland freight
Is only allowed to be deducted from the dutiable cost when-
>1. The original purchase is made from a landlocked country, so when the truck or train passes the border the **inland freight** to the port or airport of export becomes international freight.
>2. A carrier or freight forwarder offers a door/door or door/port rate, and the goods are purchased under CIF terms. In this case, as a quote from the door was offered, the entire amount can be deducted.

f. Discounts
Discounts, as long as they are taken advantage of, and their guidelines adhered to, are acceptable as deductions from the entered value. For example-
>1. Prepayment discount- This discount is acceptable to U.S. Customs as long as the buyer does indeed pay for the goods before shipment. U.S. Customs may require proof of this prepayment.
>2. Quantitative discount- This discount is acceptable to Customs as long as the quantity mandated in the discount is actually purchased.

Customs bond (surety bond)
To ensure collection of all revenues, U.S. Customs regulations require all entries valued over $2000.00 and any entry of restricted merchandise, of any value, to include a Surety Bond as a guarantee to Customs that all funds assessed on that entry be paid. Surety bonds must be obtained from a licensed and bonded surety company. Importers generally secure them through their Customhouse Broker and often cannot obtain them directly from the surety company.

Unlike the IRS, U.S. Customs does not choose to be a collection agency. If an importer fails to pay Customs any duties or charges owed to them the delinquent amount is demanded to be paid from the surety company. The surety company then attempts to track down the importer and to recover the outlaid funds.

COST OF SURETY BONDS

Yearly bond- (Estimated cost, use as a guide only!)
$500.00 for a $50,000 bond. A $50,000 bond will cover all entries per year with a total duty not exceeding $500,000.00 or a single duty exceeding $50,000.

Individual bond-
Based on (Value + Duty = V+D)
For non-restricted items- V+D at $4.00 per $1000.00. $40.00 minimum
Example: $20,000.00 value + $4,000.00 duty = $24,000.00 x 4 = $96.00

For restricted items- V+D at $12.00 per $1000. $40.00 minimum
Example: $20,000 value + $4,000 duty = $24,000 x 12 = $288.00

Insurance-

To insure cargo is not mandatory, but usually a commonsense precaution. An insurance policy can be secured by the seller, buyer, forwarder or broker. However it is obtained, the importer should be certain to have one original copy showing who is the U.S. agent, the insurance company, and who should be contacted in case of damage or loss.

Any insurance policy should be issued in an amount high enough to cover all loss of the value of the cargo, the shipping cost, duties plus 10% to cover loss of profit and sales.

Example: $30,000.00 value + $3000.00 freight + $7000.00 duty = $40,000.00
$40,000.00 + $4,000.00 (10%) = $44,000.00
POLICY VALUE- $44,000.00

Insurance policies should always protect liability for the following:
a.   Warehouse to Warehouse coverage
Any loss from door/door is covered. This avoids disputes with the insurer about where and when the loss/damage occurred.
b.   All Risk
Covers any damage or loss for any reason. Often, there will be a deductible of between $100-500 in the policy to avoid deminimus claims.
c.   Complete general average coverage
General average occurs when an ocean carrier is damaged, as well as part of the cargo laden onboard. In order to spread the loss from just one insurance company, the carrier's owner declare General Average, whereby, the loss is averaged between the carrier's owners and the owners of the undamaged cargo aboard the vessel. Before releasing the undamaged freight at its destination the carrier will request either a cash payment of the averaged loss or a copy of the insurance policy showing that they will be reimbursed from the insurance company. The amount can be quite substantial, even in the $1,000s of dollars, so having insurance with general average coverate is mandatory!

Approximate cost for insurance-

When estimating insurance for a landed cost- the following rates can be used:

Airfreight general cargo-   ½ of 1%
Ocean freight   -   General cargo-
      ½ of 1%-   Europe, Hong Kong, Taiwan Caribbean, Canada, Mexico
      1%   -   Most third world countries, Africa, Middle East

Refrigerated, autos, hazardous materials, fragile cargo and household goods from all points, add 3% to the above charges.

SELF-INSURANCE- Large importers, who can afford to suffer a complete loss of a shipment without having financial difficulties and who import cargo not easily damaged, should consider the option of self-insuring their cargo. When importers hold an insurance policy the claims are able to be paid usually within one month (if not sooner) from the date of loss. Yet the insurance company doesn't just pay out claims. Once paid, they seek out the liable party, be it the trucker, carrier, stevedore, or shipper. They attempt to be reimbursed for their loss, or at least a portion of it. Established importers with an track record of little or no loss or damage should consider self-insurance. Instead of paying an insurance company for their policy, they don't insure at all, and bank the premium normally paid to the insurer. If their record of few claims hold up, within a short period of time they should have saved enough money to pay for any claim, even a total loss. In addition, just because they do not have insurance does not stop them from litigation against the errant party and they often are able to recover damages from a loss.

THE CUSTOMSHOUSE BROKER

As previously mentioned in the chapter about freight forwarders, it is advisable whenever possible to hire one party who can be the customhouse broker, freight forwarder and arrange delivery to the ultimate destination. An importer can usually obtain substantial discounts over employing each party separately, save on transfer fees, messenger and courier charges, as well as having to call only one person to find out about the status of the shipment.

In most cases a customhouse broker's fee ranges from between $100-150 depending on the port of entry, complexity of the entry and expected volume of shipments. To estimate a landed cost when the actual fee is not known, use $100.00 per entry as a good guideline.

Customhouse brokers are licensed by the U.S. government and service importers by clearing their cargoes through Customs for them. Clearing Customs is only part of the task. Advising the importer that his paperwork is deficient BEFORE sending the entry for Customs scrutiny shows the mettle of a good broker.

What importers should do for their Customhouse Brokers-

1. Pay their bills on time.
Customhouse brokers are often asked to front out large sums of money for freight and duty, on behalf of the importer, for a low fee. Expect high quality Customs information from your broker. Do not expect them to factor your shipments.

2. Supply copies of documents in advance to the broker.
All importers should require the overseas vendor to fax them (and the broker) a set of non-negotiable documents at time of shipment. This will give the broker and the importer ample time to discover if anything is amiss and needs correction. Sending the

broker late paperwork is counterproductive and raises the incidence of errors on the broker's part because they have to process them quickly.

3. Provide the broker with any tariff classifications and rates that you have researched.
Provide the broker with as much information as possible concerning your import commodities. In addition, supply the broker with any freight rates you have negotiated with forwarders, as the broker will often outlay funds on behalf of the importer. Without knowing the rates, how does the broker know if he is overpaying your charges?

What Customhouse Brokers should provide for Importers.

1. U.S. Customhouse Brokers should educate importers to Customs laws
Brokers should analyze the documents from the importer for correctness and completeness and advise the importer at once of any remedial steps they should take.
2. Entries should be processed efficiently and accurately
Brokers should process the importer's paperwork when received, or if the documents are received far in advance of arrival, within 5 days of arrival. U.S. Customs allows Brokers to file paperwork 5 days in advance of arrival for ocean cargo, and when wheels are up for air cargo.
3. Customhouse Brokers should be available to their clients
All brokers should be responsive to importers' calls. Although anyone can be busy, or backlogged when called, any importer should expect a call back within a day. If the call is an emergency, then the importer should state this to the receptionist to leave no doubt as to the priority nature of the issue.
4. Brokers are an extension of the importer's office
A sign of a good broker is one who follows the importer's instructions and assigns a knowledgeable customer service representative to monitor each client. No one appreciates being passed around in an office from the entry clerk, to the delivery clerk to the documentation clerk to answer a single question. The broker should ALWAYS make himself available, as required by law, to oversee and monitor his office. The broker must be an active presence in the day-to-day filing of entries.
5. Another sign of a competent broker is if he processes bills promptly.
Most brokers process shipments, prepare entries and deliveries and bills at the same time. A delay in billing often signifies that the whole operation is backlogged. Once a broker's bill is received by an importer, he should also verify that the duty and freight rates are correct. Quick notification to the broker of an error enables a corrected entry being sent to Customs instead of an entry in need of correction.

The Advantage of Working with a Combination Broker/Forwarder
Many freight forwarders are also customhouse brokers, and in many situations deliver the cargo to its ultimate destination themselves. This complete service is by far the best way an importer can simplify their operation and often achieve the best combination of rates and services.

1. When the forwarder is your broker, a transfer fee for documents is eliminated. The savings $30-60 per shipment.

2. When the forwarder/broker also delivers the cargo he can provide the importer with a complete tracking system, from overseas to destination. An importer who requested regular updates of this information, by fax or e-mail, can save himself the trouble of calling the forwarder, then broker, then trucking company to find out about his cargo. In addition, these three parties can no longer blame the other for mishandling. If the job is not done correctly, the forwarder/broker is the only one who could be responsible.

3. When an importer brings cargo into more than one port he has the option of working with separate forwarders/brokers in each port, or a centralized office who can coordinate all shipments. He can achieve savings no doubt, by working with each separate office. But the convenience of working with a centralized office offers the importer more TIME to work on matters that can let his business grow, such as vendors and customers. If you can FIND A FORWARDER/BROKER YOU CAN TRUST, then STICK WITH HIM. Check his rates from time to time, but the assurance that a competent, helpful, professional is working on your behalf can free up an importer's time to make his business grow.

Trucking Companies-

If an importer arranges for his own trucking company, he should be certain that they provide him with a good service. Often the lowest rates do not mean a top service. As in any other service business, only when they perform the work does their true service become apparent. Salesmen are just that, salesmen. It is the operations and competency of the service that maintain the business. Here are certain "hints" to see whether your trucker is doing his job or not:

1. Does your trucker constantly deliver late, even a day or two later than he promised you? There are variables; long lines at piers or warehouses, city traffic, which can slow deliveries, however, able trucker should be aware of this and take them into account when giving approximate delivery times.

2. From the time the customhouse broker issues the delivery order until the cargo is picked up no more than two working days should pass, (as long as the freight has arrived.)

3. Are the trucks that deliver your cargo clean, well kept and in good road-worthy condition? (Look at the tires!)

4. Are the drivers helpful?

5. Does your regular trucker give you at least 14 days credit on bills? This is normal for the industry, especially repeat customers. It is not unusual for first time customers to have to pay for a delivery in advance, or as a C.O.D.

Examination Charges
U.S. Customs has the right to examine any and all cargo arriving in this country. The FDA, BAI and other government agencies, when the cargo falls under their jurisdiction, can order examinations also. The importer is responsible for all exam charges including charges to get the cargo to a U.S. Customs exam facility. For small shipments, estimate an exam charge of $100. For full containers estimate a charge of $750. When calculating projected landed cost, always include exam charges. If the exam does not occur, it increases the profit margin.

It would be almost impossible to examine all merchandise arriving in this country. U.S. Customs examines merchandise for contraband, so that cargo imported from areas that produce drugs are always subject to a higher rate of examination that cargo from areas not actively involved in the narcotics trade. In addition to contraband examination, cargo is examined to verify that the information supplied on the Customs entry is accurate or when the description of the merchandise on the entry is of insufficient detail. Shipments of first time importers are usually subject to exam, as no track record exists for these importers. U.S. Customs maintains data banks on all importers, detailing their entry history and ability to comply with the Customs regulations of the United States. Importers who have suppliers issue invoices with incorrect or incomplete information, fail to mark cargo with the required country of origin in proper fashion, and show a general disregard for Customs bills, requests for information, and notices of action can expect to have most, if not all of their shipments examined.

Certain exams are unavoidable, and a necessary expense in importing. Importers must research correct classification, complete invoice descriptions for incoming cargo and legal marking of merchandise advising their foreign vendors of the regulations and all requirements. Furthermore, stipulating on these findings on all purchase orders and letters of credits can only serve the importer by proving to U.S. Customs that they take their regulations seriously and force compliance by their vendors. There is no doubt that importers who act accordingly will be rewarded with reduced examinations (save the unavoidable contraband exam). However, have no doubt that periodically U.S. Customs will examine even the most conscientious importer's cargo, often with exams of 3-4 consecutive shipments. Sometimes, in error, these exams continue for no reason. The remedy would be for the customhouse broker or importer to write the District Director at the port of entry. Don't question Customs' right to examine a shipment, but that the importer has no known faults (with their import cargoes) and ask that Customs reconsider the need to continually examine their imports. If a problem exists, they will surely be notified of it. If not, perhaps a quirk in the U.S. Customs computer system caused the problem, and the exams will stop soon after.

Fumigation Charges
Importers should be aware of what merchandise often requires fumigation, and always consider these charges when calculating the landed cost. Most brass items from India

require fumigation as does marble and stone products, which attract snails. Pallets and wood crating must be free from pests or require fumigation. While fumigation of wood packing from China is mandatory, discovery of pests upon arrival can result in additional fumigation in the United States. Packing must never be hay or straw. When discovered, all hay and straw must be removed (it may contain Hoof and Mouth virus) and replaced with conventional packing. After incinerating the culprits, the total cost can run into the thousands of dollars, even for a small shipment.

Banking fees- When purchasing cargo under a letter of credit, most banks charges a fee plus a commission on total letter of credit amount. For landed cost purposes, estimate $50.00 per letter of credit, plus ½ of 1% for the commission.

Example- $50,000 Letter of Credit
   $50 (flat fee) + $250 (1/2 of 1%)= $300.00 fee.

The importer should also be aware that once a letter of credit is opened, his assets equal to the amount of the letter of credit are held pending the letter of credit's completion.

======================

CHAPTER SIX

The Correct and Complete Method
For Issuing a Purchase Order

ALWAYS NEGOTIATE BEFORE ISSUING A PURCHASE ORDER!

An American importer finds a product that he feels he can import legally into the U.S. and resell for a profit over the cost of the merchandise and the total expense of getting it into his warehouse. The foreign vendor will push the importer to issue a purchase order. A purchase order is the first confirmation to the vendor that the importer is serious and is committed to purchase the goods. Purchase orders must be taken seriously as they are, for all intents and purposes, a commitment to buy the merchandise mentioned therein. It is for that reason that all negotiations between the buyer and seller must be settled before the purchase order is actually issued. **The purchase order is the finale of those negotiations, not the beginning.**

A foreign vendor will either offer prices via fax, or send a catalog detailing his merchandise. In many cases, the seller expects to negotiate, if not cost, other aspects of the transaction. One can expect the vendor to give a complete breakdown of packing specification, including weight and measures, so that the potential buyer can calculate exactly how much (in weight and size) he is ordering. The exchange of faxes has become the standard means of negotiating international purchases. In the future e-mail will likely become more and more prevalent.

Points to Negotiate, or at least clarify, before placing a purchase order

1. Price
The price offered by the vendor will be accompanied by a terms of sale, (per dozen $30.00 FOB Milan, or $35.00 CIF Atlanta). This price can often be negotiated lower for one of the following three factors:

a). Prepayment discount
Offered to lure the importer to pay for the goods before they leave the country of export, the buyer's reward is a percentage discount, usually 3% to 5%. This should only be accepted if the seller is well known to the importer, or the prepayment occurs when the cargo is delivered to the

importer's forwarder in the country of exportation. NEVER agree to this when funds are at risk.

b). Quantity discount
If you agree to buy a specific large quantity of goods a discount of between 3%-6% is not uncommon.

c). First time purchaser discount
When buying from a vendor for the first time, he might be persuaded to offer a discount, hoping to gain a new and regular customer. For the importer to claim that he currently buys the same product elsewhere can push the supplier to agree to such a reduction.

2. Quality
Unless the foreign seller's products are of the same or better quality that you can buy elsewhere, it is foolish to purchase them. Always request a sample, or group of samples before finally deciding to purchase any item in large quantities. Try to get the vendor to agree to repay any cost for the samples (and the cost to send them to the U.S.) by deducting these expenses from the first order. When buying from a new vendor, it is often important to have the goods checked for quality BEFORE shipping. A forwarder's overseas agent can usually perform the test (or hire a company to have the test performed) for quality BEFORE the goods leave the country of export. If they are not up to quality, it makes no sense to ship them. An importer should be certain that any purchase order dictate that their own quality control expert examine the goods, and a letter stating that these goods are of the required quality be a requirement before the goods are shipped. Should the goods be of an inferior quality, but still acceptable, additional negotiations to obtain a lower cost are in order.

3. Quantity
As detailed in #1, also check if you can obtain a quantitative discount from the vendor. But, quantities being ordered should also be checked to see if they are in stock or have to be manufactured before shipment. This can seriously effect a time-sensitive purchase.

4. Availability
When the goods can be ready to be shipped can effect a sale and the purchase price. Be sure to confirm with the vendor when the goods can be manufactured if they are not available for immediate shipment. Don't forget to add this time on to the transit time to the U.S. and then only if this time frame still is suitable should any order be placed.

5. Terms of Sale
Various prices may be offered along with a change in terms of sale. Depending on the item, the FOB price can be 3-10% lower than the CIF terms.

6. Mode of Transport

When a purchase is made under EX-WORKS or FOB terms the importer designates the mode of transport and the forwarder. There is no negotiation. The goods are shipped according to the importer's wishes.

However, when buying under CIF, CIFDDP, or CIFDP terms the importer must find out from the seller the means and method for shipping the goods, such as air or ocean, direct or transshipped, the fast vessel or the literal, slow boat from China. A good example is shipping from any Chinese port to the East Coast of the United States. A CIF New York purchase could mean a 60-day transit time with a very slow line, or a 15-day transit time with a rapid one. On CIF purchases always have the seller spell out the TRANSIT TIME & FREQUENCY OF SAILING. For air shipments, whether or not the goods are shipped on direct flights.

7. Latest Shipping Date

This date is shown on the bill of lading or airway bill, as the date the cargo is exported from the foreign country. It is important to specify latest permitted shipping date on time-sensitive merchandise, especially wearing apparel and holiday goods (Christmas, Halloween, etc.)

8. Shipping Specifications

These specifications, such as weight and measure, are important, especially when trying to fill a container to its limit in both size and weight (see page 44 for container sizes). Although the seller provides the shipping sizes in his original sales brochure it is important to communicate with the seller, who probably has shipped full containers in other instances. He can advise exactly how much cargo should be ordered to fill a container. If pallets and shrink wrapping of cargo is required the importer may request, as a point of negotiation, that these costs and expenses to not only be included on the original invoice, but that their expense be absorbed by the vendor, instead of as an additional charge.

9. Shipping Notification

It is important for importers to insist that the seller notify the buyer when and how the goods are shipped. This is especially important if the terms of sale are CIF, since the importer's forwarder is no longer keeping tabs of the shipment. The following statement, added to the purchase order, will mandate correct notification.

> *"The seller must inform the importer via fax, one week prior to actual shipping, of the intended shipping date, as well as fax confirmation that the goods were sent after the fact."*

The sellers tend not to notify the importer unless formally requested to do so.

10. Marking Requirements-
As mentioned in Chapter II, both U.S. Customs and other government agencies have marking requirements. Even if an imported product is exempt from any marking, the outside package (crate, box, drum) which it is shipped in must be marked showing the country of origin. In some cases, such as certain plumbing supplies and tools, the country of origin marking has to be "etched, die-cast or engraved" into each item. Be certain in the purchase order to state plainly the required marking guidelines for the seller. His confirmation of the purchase order will cite his concurrence. The buyer must also advise the seller of specific shipping marks, to distinguish the cargo from any others being sent. The importer does not have to use his full name, but purchase order number part number, or abbreviated company name are not unusual shipping marks to have stenciled on the outside package.

11. Specific Invoice Requirements
One of the major reasons that goods are mis-classified, or slated for a commodity examination is that the invoice does not describe the item in sufficient detail for Customs to classify under the Harmonized System. Therefore, it is up to the importer to provide the description to the seller, in words similar to the description in the harmonized tariff. One example; the importer of hardware products can insist *"the vendor will describe on the commercial invoice (bill of sale) as- item#-123B3 as a 100% brass door knob, with key."* Left to his own direction, or perhaps because of a language barrier, the uninformed seller might describe the same item as- **"KNOBS-#123B3"** which tells the importer and U.S. Customs nothing. The result: probably the costs and delays of a Customs examination.

12. Documentation Requirements
Usual document requirements of any seller are-
   1). Detailed commercial invoice (in triplicate)
   2). Complete packing list
   3). Shipping document (bill of lading or air waybill)
However, after making inquiries with U.S. Customs and other government agencies (when necessary) an importer often determines that special documentation is needed in order to import the cargo into the United States. The importer **MUST** confirm that the seller can provide this documentation, and that it is included in the cost quoted. If it is not included in the cost, the importer should have the seller provide him with the cost breakdown to provide the required documents.
   4). When buying from China (and Hong Kong) either a statement by the importer noting, "no wood packing" or a fumigation certificate.

13. Packing Materials
In most cases the seller provides adequate packing for the article to be shipped internationally. However, inferior packing is cheaper than sturdy packing. Some sellers will use the cheapest packing material to save costs unless the exact required method of packing is dictated to them, in writing, by the importer. The vendor can often palletize

and/or shrink-wrap the cartons but may not because they are not requested to do so, or do not want to bear the additional expense. If the importer knows that the only way to avoid damage during the international shipping is to have the goods palletized and shrink-wrapped, it should be a matter of negotiation. All matters of packing MUST be ironed out before placing a purchase order.

14. Method of Payment

The method that the seller needs to be paid, and how the importer prefers to pay for the cargo must be ironed out before issuing the purchase order.   Some manufacturers need a letter of credit to discount, so they can obtain funds for the raw materials to manufacture the purchase. On the other hand, the importer must be aware that the letter of credit is the only means of paying for the shipment so as to include this expense in the projected landed cost.

Items that cannot be negotiated.

The foreign vendor may have certain items that are nonnegotiable. So may the importer. The seller may require a letter of credit and allow no other method of payment. He can insist on a CIF purchase. Conversely the importer will also have items that he must insist upon, such as U.S. Customs regulations that are matters of law so that they leave no room for negotiation. There will be many other points that both parties have the ability to bend on. Each party should make clear, to avoid a needless waste of time, which points are etched in stone and which are not. Each party should then realize the other's needs and desires and both should find a middle ground. If this middle ground can be found, business can be done. Goods can be bought and sold, but only due to a mutual respect of both parties for the other's needs.   Often, relationships between the foreign vendor and American importer can go on for years IF NOT DECADES!

Each party must consider that they are dealing with a different culture with the same goal: more business is good business. Often it is a language barrier that sabotages a negotiation. If the importer feels that this is occurring, they should seek the help of their forwarder, whose agent not only speaks the same language, but is located close to the seller. This is another point in considering the importance of an FOB purchase, it gives the importer a representative in the foreign country, who can act on his behalf.

Other Important Stipulations

The foreign vendor must provide, on the commercial invoice or on an attachment to the commercial invoice, the following statements, as well as a signature of a responsible party at his company and that person's title.

1. I certify that the price of these goods stated on invoice _____ (or this invoice) is the price that these goods were sold for, and no rebate, assist, additional payment or

gratuity, in either funds or any assets has been paid by the buyer in an effort to reduce the cost shown on the invoice.

2. I certify that these goods were not made by any penal or prison institution or by slave labor.

3. I certify that any wood used in this shipment, or in the packing materials is free from bark and has been kiln dried, to reduce the risk of any pests or eggs of pests being present.

4. I certify that these products are the growth, manufacture and produce of _____ country, and they were not shipped to an intermediate country and relabeled. There is no intent on my part as seller of these goods to violate any law of the United States of America with reference to transshipment of freight from one country to another, with the ultimate goal of reducing duty rates or mis-declaring the country of origin. In summation the cost, terms of sale, and country of origin are correct as described on this invoice.

5. I certify that all packing charges, including the labor of packing and the packing material are included in the cost of the merchandise.

(A signature, title and date of a responsible person at the foreign seller's company must be affixed to the bottom of this document)

Finally, THE PURCHASE ORDER

Only when the importer and foreign seller are in agreement on the proposed transaction should the importer issue a purchase order. The purchase order is the culmination of negotiations not the beginning. A correctly issued purchase order will, in most cases, result in the goods being manufactured, packed and shipped in the manner prescribed by the importer. In other words, the importer has taken CONTROL of the purchase, and is buying the merchandise of the quality he needs, at the cost he is willing to pay and at the time he needs them. ALL IN ACCORDANCE WITH THE CUSTOMS REGULATIONS OF THE UNITED STATES OF AMERICA.

NEVER issue a purchase order until all matters are resolved. Problems grow from misunderstandings and topics left in the dark. If all items are ironed out in advance, then the major disagreements that jeopardize current and future business transactions will be few and far between.

A Complete Purchase Order
Issuing an incomplete purchase order invites the foreign seller to take advantage of the situation. The smartest way to issue a purchase order is to issue a complete purchase order that protects the importer. By complete, I am referring to one that:

1. Lets the importer take control of the shipment.

2. Allows no gray areas. Furnishes enough information so the buyer and the seller are in agreement, and are aware of each other's responsibilities in the transaction.

3. FOB and EX-WORKS shipments allow the IMPORTER'S freight forwarder to be nominated, who the foreign seller can contact to arrange shipment of the goods. The freight forwarder in the U.S. can furnish the name of their overseas counterpart with full details (phone, fax, contact, address).

4. Always show latest allowed date of shipment.

5. Instructs the seller how to make up the commercial invoice. When necessary instructs the seller in how to describe the item to conform with all Customs requirements.

6. Makes sure your purchase order details any additional information that Customs will require in simple terms such as- SELLER will provide x,y,z. Packing specifications and requirements must be included. These details should have been worked out before actually issuing the purchase order, so confirmation should be a "rubber stamp."

7. ALWAYS add the statements shown on page- 68, concerning proper packing, slave and convict labor, and other confirmations.

CHAPTER SEVEN

The Paying for Imported Merchandise

CORRECT STEPS OF INTERNATIONAL PURCHASING

The following six points detail the correct method of purchasing cargo internationally, resulting in a satisfied seller and buyer.

1. Seller and buyer negotiate.
2. Purchase order is issued.
3. Purchase order is confirmed by seller. Seller will request how the merchandise is to be paid for.
4. Buyer and seller work out how the goods will be paid for.
5. A letter of credit, telex transfer or other means of exchanging funds for the goods is transmitted.
6. The importer, having fully prepared for the shipment, gets the goods when he wants them, at the cost he wants them, with little or no Customs or carrier problems

Paying for goods internationally is totally different than paying for them domestically. Importers, especially when purchasing goods from a foreign vendor for the first time, are concerned that they will lose their money. Seller's priority, on the other hand, is that they will not get paid for their goods. Each must agree to a method which will satisfy both parties. Three examples that can serve this purpose are:

1. Pre-payment + C.O.D.

Pre-payment can be used only when the importer purchases the goods under terms of sale FOB or Ex-works. It is also recommended only for smaller shipments, as the buyer is basically paying for the goods in advance. On larger purchases, if pre-payment is suggested, the importer should at least get a discount for extending his money ahead of time. On the other hand, no seller will ship goods internationally under COD terms. What guarantee does he have that the money will be paid when the cargo arrives overseas. COD can only be used when the importer sends a draft or telex transfer to his freight forwarder's agent in the country of export. At the time of transfer of cargo, the goods are turned over to the importer's forwarder's agent. The money is only transferred when the cargo is accepted. The agent then exchanges the funds for the goods. The importer, through use of his forwarder's agent, has extended his influence overseas, and is in possession of the goods at time of transfer of funds. Most agents charge a fee

($50.00) for the COD, whereas the telex transfer is a direct exchange between the importer and foreign seller.

2. Telex Transfer

This method of payment is useful in eliminating letter of credit fees, however, the seller and buyer must have some previous relationship, as a degree of trust is involved. The following steps cannot be acceptable for the importer unless the merchandise is purchased under an FOB or ex-works terms of sale. The importer is only safeguarded by nominating his own freight forwarder.

> 1. The seller transfers the cargo over to the importer's forwarder's foreign agent in exchange for the negotiable bills of lading consigned to the order of the shipper, thereby withholding legal right of the merchandise until he actually gets paid.
> 2. Once in possession of the on-board bills of lading, showing that the goods have actually been shipped, the seller faxes a copy of the bill of lading to the importer. The importer can double check the information with his forwarder, verifying that the cargo has left the country of export.
> 3. Assured that the cargo is shipped, the importer telex transfers the funds to the seller who, upon receipt, (or bank confirmation that the funds were sent) couriers the shipping documents (bill of lading, invoice, packing list and any other required document) to the importer. The seller is paid. The importer can claim the cargo with the original documents.

The risk is present two ways. First, what if after being paid the seller does not send the original documents to the importer. To protect his interest, the importer must receive a statement from the seller that, if he (the importer) can prove that he has paid for the goods the freight forwarder will release the cargo automatically to the importer. The seller is at risk in that, what if the importer does not pay him, and the seller gives the goods to the importer without payment. The seller's recourse is to commence litigation against the forwarder, who under maritime law, must follow the instructions of the shipper, and is liable to pay the shipper if he illegally releases the cargo. The importer should also insist that the seller fax copies of all required documents, as well as turn over one set to the freight forwarder.

Letters of Credit (L/C).

A letter of credit is a formal, legal, binding agreement between the importer and foreign seller, whereby the seller gets paid for the merchandise once the stipulations on the letter of credit are met. The bank of the buyer **(issuing bank)** and the bank of the seller **(advising bank)** serve as literal go-betweens; the issuing bank holding the funds until the documents granting legal title (bill of lading) arrive, the advising bank turning the funds over to the seller.

BASICS OF THE LETTER OF CREDIT

1. Importance of the Application
The buyer begins by obtaining a letter of credit application from the **issuing bank**. The importer must be certain to put on the application **ALL REQUIREMENTS** already indicated on the purchase order. These stipulations guarantee that the goods will be shipped when he wants them to be, and that the letter of credit will have all documents needed for clearance. On FOB and EX-WORKS shipments the letter of credit will also specify the shipping agent. These are the same variables that have been worked out before the purchase order was issued. Having fully stated them on the purchase order, with the seller agreeing to them on the purchase order confirmation, the letter of credit smoothly follows suit.

2. Transmission of the Letter of Credit
The issuing bank accepts the application, issues a letter of credit number, and will insist that the amount of the letter of credit be deposited in the bank and held as security, until the requirements of the letter of credit are met by the **advising bank.** The letter of credit is then forwarded overseas to the advising bank who notifies the seller that the letter of credit has arrived and the terms of the letter of credit stated therein.

The foreign seller often needs the funds guaranteed by the letter of credit, and the advising bank will discount the total by 3% to 5%, then allowing creditworthy sellers to gain access to the funds to purchase raw materials to manufacture the cargo.

3. Return of the Letter of Credit to the Issuing Bank
After the goods are produced, all documents are presented to the advising bank who makes sure that there are no discrepancies between the documents and the letter of credit. The advising bank forwards the documents to the issuing bank, who notifies the importer that the letter of credit has been received from overseas, and examines it for any discrepancies, which would be any error in the presentation from the original application. If there are no discrepancies, the letter of credit is automatically accepted and funds transferred from the importer's account, in exchange for the shipping documents that allow the importer to claim the cargo.

4. Working with Discrepancies
Any discrepancy with the letter of credit allows a refusal by the importer. Discrepancies are literally **ANY ERROR, MISTAKE, MISSPELLING, MISSING DOCUMENT or FAILURE TO ADHERE TO ANY STIPULATION.** In lieu of refusal the importer has two other options.

1. Waive the discrepancy as being insignificant.
2. Renegotiate the amount of the letter of credit to compensate him for any loss due to the discrepancy.

Acceptable discrepancies
Sometimes there will be a discrepancy that is agreeable to the importer. When the importer suffers no real hardship, loss of business or actual financial loss for the discrepancy the importer should, without second thought, accept the L/C. An importer who uses an insignificant discrepancy as a reason to force the seller to reduce his costs leaves himself open for retaliation in the future. Why jeopardize a possible lifetime relationship to make a few dollars off of your trading partner's mistake? Often the seller will pre-advise the importer of the discrepancy, and ask him to confirm that he will waive it. The alternative is to amend the letter of credit, resulting in higher banking charges. Each discrepancy should be analyzed for its own merit and acted upon accordingly.

Unacceptable discrepancies
Some discrepancies are never acceptable. Late presentation can cause storage fees upon arrival into the United States, and perhaps loss of sales as a result of the delay. The importer must, in this case, negotiate with the seller a reduction in the letter of credit amount, as compensation.

A worse discrepancy is when a required Customs document is not present, such as a visa or license. Unable to clear the shipment, the importer should not accept the L/C no matter how much of a reduction the vendor offers. It makes no sense to own the cargo without the ability to clear the cargo through Customs. Unless the importer has a buyer overseas, and can negotiate a substantial reduction in the cost, refusing the shipment is the ONLY option.

Bank Guarantee
In the event a letter of credit becomes lost in banking channels, the bank can issue a guarantee which will be acceptable to the carrier or forwarder in lieu of the original bill of lading. This will satisfy the carrier but the importer MUST BE CERTAIN THAT NO MISSING DOCUMENT, OR LATE QUOTA PRESENTATION WILL KEEP HIM FROM CLEARING CUSTOMS! The carrier/forwarder may be satisfied, but not Customs. A bank will only issue a guarantee if the importer agrees, in doing so, to pay for the shipment and waive any discrepancies present in the L/C when it finally is located. Note also, if the bank is the one who loses the papers, don't let the bank charge for the guarantee!

Safeguarding the Letter of Credit
One essential clause in any letter of credit is to have the letter of credit sent by courier from the advising bank to the issuing bank once it is complete. Without this stipulation, the advising bank is under no obligation how to send the documents overseas. Sent regular mail, the importer is doomed to hardship. The importer can provide his courier particulars (DHL, FedEx, AIRBORNE, etc.) particulars on the letter of credit and insist that the courier be used to transfer the documents. The cost for this messenger is small compared to the loss and delay of the cargo should the letter of credit be sent regular mail.

Safeguarding essential documents outside of the Letter of Credit

Irreplaceable or highly important documents (such as an export license or visa necessary for clearance) should never be sent with the letter of credit. In lieu of a requirement for the original document, the following should be the stipulation on the Letter of Credit:

   a). Photocopy of original document.

   b). Statement from seller that the original document was sent to the importer via courier pouch # _____.

Back-to-back Letters of Credit

Of great advantage to the importer is when a domestic company issues a letter of credit to an importer. The funds posted by this third party letter of credit can be used when the letter of credit specifies that a back-to-back letter of credit is permissible. The funds from the originally issued letter of credit are used as collateral for the new letter of credit alleviating the importer's need to finance the shipment. A back-to-back letter of credit may have specific requirements, such as both letter of credits must reflect the same terms of sale. Any importer not familiar with back-to-back letters of credit is encouraged to work with a knowledgeable forwarder or broker as an adviser.

CHAPTER EIGHT

Hints, Miscellany, Options, Audit Preparation
And Summary

SIX HINTS FOR A SUCCESSFUL IMPORT

1. Always research a potential import in advance
Be certain that the product is allowed entry into this country, that it is legal to import from the country where the cargo was manufactured, produced or grown, and calculate the landed cost to be certain that a loss is not suffered.

2. Be Sure To Contact U.S. Customs Before Ordering Merchandise
U.S. Customs offers free advise on required documents, legality of admission of cargo, duty and classification and also if other government agencies are concerned with the commodity being imported.

3. If Customs Indicates Other Government Agencies Have an Interest in your import, CONTACT THOSE AGENCIES
Other agencies may require licensing, special documents and permits. The shipper must confirm that these requirements can be satisfied by the shipper before placing a purchase order.

4. By Purchasing Under Terms of Sale FOB (or Ex-Works) the importer can keep better control over his import
Purchasing under FOB (or Ex-Works) allows the importer to designate who and how the cargo is to be shipped to the United States. Appointing his own forwarding agent, he is able to monitor the departure and arrival of the cargo as well as pre-establishing a rate for the transport.

5. The importer is best advised to assign one shipping agent, to arrange complete transportation from overseas to the ultimate destination in the United States
Instead of having to contact separate forwarders, truckers and customhouse brokers the importer needs only one reliable, responsible and honest contact. He allows this party to handle all his import arrangements, requiring the importer only to periodically audit the agent's service and rates.

6. Always Completely Finish Negotiations with the Foreign Vendor before Placing the Purchase Order
NEVER place a purchase order until all costs, legality and negotiations with the foreign shipper are assured correct and completed. A running dialogue should lead up to the purchase order, not to amend it repeatedly subsequently to purchase.

These six points are the basis from which successful international purchasing begins. Each one is discussed in greater detail earlier in this booklet, and any information not covered and needed should be obtained by the experts in the field who have acquired the knowledge over many years. The importer should use the bulk of his time on sourcing new markets, locating new vendors and in sales projections to sell his wares. However, the basics must be learned by the importer for two reasons. First, how can he pick a forwarder, or obtain rate quotes, or hold an intelligent conversation with a Customs official without understanding basic principles upon which this knowledge is based? Second, U.S. Customs has required that all importers have a sufficient knowledge of importing to avoid violating Customs regulations through ignorance or lack of preparation, care and knowledge.

THE CUSTOMS AUDIT

Importers do not need a license to import cargo into the United States. However, if they do not obey Customs regulations they can face stiff fines and even jail sentences. U.S. Customs keeps an eye on all importers through three basic methods.

1. Review of entry documentation submitted at time of entry. The documents should be accurate, complete and meet all requirements of law. If they do not, Customs will certainly look further and press the importer to bring his documents into conformity.

2. Customs examines imported cargo to see that the merchandise matches the documentation. Should it differ, especially when Customs revenues or laws are affected negatively, the importer will be subject to repeated examinations of both cargo and documents.

3. To completely review documents, and an importer's internal procedures, U.S. Customs will at random conduct a Customs audit. Audits are conducted at an importers premise. They are not unannounced. The importer will be called in advance to make an appointment. They CANNOT be postponed repeatedly without arousing Customs justified suspicions. When contacted for the appointment, the importer will be given a list of entries that U.S. Customs wants to review with the importer at the audit.

PRINCIPLE TOPICS COVERED BY AUDITS

1. Protecting the Revenue of the United States

U.S. Customs is the largest revenue producer for the U.S. Government besides the IRS. Duty rates are not guesswork, they can be ascertained through logical use of the Rules of Interpretation of the Harmonized Schedules of the United States (HSUS). Importers should never reduce duties through many illegal activities such as mis-declaring the merchandise, claiming the goods are produced in a country with a free duty status when it is not and by lowering the entered value of the merchandise.

2. Transshipment

The United States establishes duty rates and quota regulations based on the country where merchandise is grown, produced or manufactured. Unscrupulous importers will try to mis-declare goods as being the country of origin more favorable to quota regulations and/or lower duty rates. Such activity is highly illegal. Importers who assist foreign vendors in illegal transshipment can be subject to:

1. Fines up to 300% of the domestic value of the merchandise.
2. Imprisonment.

Any documentation showing that the importer is allowing the seller to illegally transship the imported merchandise can be used as evidence against the importer. All importers should instruct their staff not to agree to any form of transshipment by e-mail or fax, and when in doubt to check with their Customhouse broker or attorney to see if they are being an unwilling party to transshipment. Note the following example:

> A foreign vendor usually ships wearing apparel from China but the quota closes. He asks the importer, via fax, if he can ship the goods from China to a sister company in American Samoa, have them relabeled and then shipped to the United States. Concurrence to this request leaves the importer subject to the penalties stated above.

3. Informed Compliance (of Importers) with Customs regulations

U.S. Customs also visits importers to check the importer's knowledge of regulations and laws relating to their merchandise. Part of the responsibility of being an importer is to have a working knowledge of Customs procedures, so as to assure Customs that merchandise will be imported under law.

Some of the documentation and literature that Customs will request to view are:

Vendor's Sales Catalogs

Offered merchandise detailed with prices, and descriptions of use and composition of material.

Communications documenting pre-purchase order negotiations

All exchanges of communication between buyer and seller are subject to Customs audit. They reveal how the final import entry evolved from the initial contact. All notations of phone conversations, letters, copies of e-mails and faxes should detail a systematic negotiation to arrive at the final purchase price and terms of sale. Variations, such as a sudden unsupported drop in price will trigger future investigations.

The Importer's Complete PO (Purchase Order) and the Sellers PO Confirmation

The shipper's documentation as well as the forwarder's bill of lading

The shipper must issue the usual documentation required by U.S. Customs and their payment documents. These are a detailed commercial invoice (in English), a packing list, as well as any specially required documents required for entry.

The Customs Entry, Delivery Order (copy) and any and all Customs correspondence related to this file

The entry must be obtained from the Customhouse Broker. The delivery order reveals the ultimate destination and any special criterion, hazardous material information, gross weights and description of merchandise. No Customhouse Broker can deny the importer a copy of the entry, as it is a requirement for the importer's master file.

Proof of payment

The importer must retain a copy of his canceled check, draft or bank statement from the letter of credit payment. This amount should correspond with the commercial invoice and letter of credit.

The importer's records - Organized files

Importers are required to retain their records for 5 years from the date of entry. The importer should maintain a cross-reference system with products, Customs entry number, and supplier. After 5 years the records are best incinerated or shredded to avoid viewing by competitors. But they should be easily accessible for the five years. Warehousing is permitted off premise. Before closing a file, a checklist should be maintained to ensure that the documents are present at time of the file's closure, as it is of greater difficulty to obtain them later on.

Internal audit - A Necessary Tool

U.S. Customs conducts audits looking for discrepancies in the paperwork, such as a variation between the commercial invoice and amount of the L/C. The importer should mimic Customs audit procedures and be sure that each importation has a complete paper trail. The purchase order leads to its confirmation followed by proof of payment, the actual invoice and a copy of the Customs entry. Whenever possible, obtain a binding ruling to be certain that the tariff classification is accurate.

Summation

Always import with confidence. An undertaking such as importing must be taken systematically with no divergence from the rules and regulations outlined in Title 19 of the Customs regulations. By using the landed cost system in this book, the importer can accurately predict his final cost per item, usually within a 5% variation. Never hesitate to consult with the experts when unclear, or indecisive on any matter.

APPENDIX

Be certain your broker provides you a copy with his invoice. Always verify entered
value, currency, classification and duty paid. When in doubt call your broker.

A commercial invoice should be provided by the foreign vendor detailing cost, terms
of sale, detailed description, his address and full particulars

When a commercial invoice is not available an importer or broker can complete
a pro forma invoice and use in place of the commercial invoice for clearance.

Upon receipt of this form via mail, the importer is encouraged to answer completely
to all questions and within 30 days. NEVER fail to respond to a Customs request.
If request is not understood, consult your broker or all U.S. Customs!

Customs will issue a notice of action after decided to usually rate or value advance an
entry, or feel it should be under a different classification. Upon receipt of this form
check with your broker to see if they believe the notice is correct. If you disagree with
the notice a protest may be filed within 90 days of liquidation for any reason.

In most cases U.S. Customs will issue this courtesy notice upon liquidation of an entry.
If the two amounts are equal then the entry was accepted as entered. If the amounts
differ consult your Customs Broker to see if he agrees with the change. Options are
open to protest a liquidation. Note this is a courtesy notice, Customs is under no obligation to issue this notice. All entries after liquidation are posted at the Customshouse.

Upon receipt of this notice the importer should contact his broker at once. This notice
alerts the importer that his merchandise was found to be not legally marked with the
country of origin and orders the import to mark it within 30 days or redeliver it to Customs
custody. Importers should only sign this notice after the goods have been marked to
conform to marking regulations and NOT before. Never ignore receipt of this notice.

List of Customs Exemptions from Marking   95

Most merchandise has to be marked with the country of origin. In some cases marking can be waived by Customs. A list of some examples follow. It is suggested to contact Customs to verify that the item is indeed exempted from marking, not just to assume that the marking is not required.

Notice to Addressee of Arrival of Mail Shipment   96

Upon receipt of this notice, contact your Customs broker at once. If not responded to within 30 days the package is automatically returned to the sender as unclaimed.

Notice of Penalty or Liquidated Damages   97

Customs will notify the importer of any penalty or liquidated damages on this form. Importers are encouraged to petition for relief from damages should they either disagree with the action or feel that their are mitigating circumstances.

PROTEST   98

This form is used to protest an entry after liquidation. This form is traditionally filed by the Customs Broker who filed entry or by a Customs attorney.

LANDED COST WORKSHEET   99

Before importing any shipment it is important to calculate, on paper, the landed cost. A landed cost takes the original cost overseas and based on the terms of sale calculates all additional charges to get the merchandise to its ultimate destination in the United States.

USING AND UNDERSTANDING THE HARMONIZED TARIFF OF THE U.S.

Appendix #1 reveals a random page from the Harmonized tariff that can be used as an example in understanding the entire tariff. Before attempting classification, read the rules of interpretation at the beginning, as well as the chapter notes at the beginning of each chapter. The tariff is divided into 100 chapters, the captioned portion above is from Chapter 82, page 3.

8203 is the heading for imports of Files, rasps, pliers, (including Cutting pliers), pincers, tweezers, metal cutting shears, etc.

8203.10.30 – subheading for files rasps not over 11 centimeters in length.
8203.10.30 – subheading for files rasps between 11 and 17 centimeters in length.

Always read the tariff from left to right, for example, after deciding that your imported item is classified under heading of 8203, your next determination would be:

Is it a file under 8203.10? Is it a plier under 8203.20? Is it a metal cutting shear under 8203.30?

For example, if you imported Slip Joint Pliers 19 centimeters in length, they would be classified under 8203.20.40.00 not under 8203.10.90.00. 8203.10.90.00 is only for files and rasps over 17 centimeters in length, not pliers. **A description of a subheading NEVER overrides the heading description. Always read the tariff from left to right, NEVER right to left.**

Units of quantity are statistical information required by Customs for the Department of Commerce. If importing files and rasps the vendor should state the "dozen" quantity on the commercial invoice. When importing tweezers the number is a requirement. In some instances, having knowledge of the net weight in kilos can also be required.

General Rates of Duty are duty rates for imports from most countries in the world. Special rates are reduced rates for items made in countries afforded special duty treatment, such as Mexico, Canada, Caribbean nations, underdeveloped nations, and Israel. While all these countries have lower duty on some items, they may not have reduced duty rates on all items. Each country and classification should be researched individually.

Column 2 rates are punitive rates on imports from Afghanistan, Cuba Laos, North Korea, and Vietnam. Note that products of Cuba are completely prohibited.

Heading/ Subheading	Stat. Suf- fix	Article Description	Units of Quantity	Rates of Duty 1 General	Rates of Duty 1 Special	Rates of Duty 2
8203		Files, rasps, pliers (including cutting pliers), pincers, tweezers, metal cutting shears, pipe-cutters, bolt cutters, perforating punches and similar handtools, and base metal parts thereof:				
8203.10		Files, rasps and similar tools:				
8203.10.30	00	Not over 11 cm in length................	doz.....	Free		47.5¢/doz.
8203.10.60	00	Over 11 cm but not over 17 cm in length..	doz.....	Free		62.5¢/doz.
8203.10.90	00	Over 17 cm in length.....................	doz.....	Free		77.5¢/doz.
8203.20		Pliers (including cutting pliers), pincers, tweezers and similar tools, and parts thereof:				
8203.20.20	00	Tweezers...............................	No......	4%	Free (A,CA,E,IL,J, MX)	60%
		Other:				
8203.20.40	00	Slip joint pliers..................	doz.....	12%	Free (A+,CA,E,IL, J) 4.8% (MX) \	60%
8203.20.60		Other (except parts)................	....	12¢/doz. + 5.5%	Free (A,CA,E,IL,J, MX)	$1.20/doz. + 60%
	30	Pliers........................	doz.			
	60	Other.........................	doz.			
8203.20.80	00	Parts..............................	X.......	4.5%	Free (A,CA,E,IL,J, MX)	45%
8203.30.00	00	Metal cutting shears and similar tools, and parts thereof................................	No......	Free		50%
8203.40		Pipe cutters, bolt cutters, perforating punches and similar tools, and parts thereof:				
8203.40.30	00	With cutting part containing by weight over 0.2 percent of chromium, molybdenum, or tungsten or over 0.1 percent of vanadium................................	X.......	6%	Free (A,CA,E,IL,J, MX)	60%
8203.40.60	00	Other (including parts)................	X.......	3.3%	Free (A,CA,E,IL,J, MX)	50%
8204		Hand-operated spanners and wrenches (including torque meter wrenches but not including tap wrenches); socket wrenches, with or without handles, drives or extensions; base metal parts thereof:				
		Hand-operated spanners and wrenches, and parts thereof:				
8204.11.00		Nonadjustable, and parts thereof.........	....	9%	Free (A,CA,E,IL,J, MX)	45%
	30	Open-end, box and combination open-end and box wrenches...........	No.			
	60	Other (including parts).............	X			
8204.12.00	00	Adjustable, and parts thereof............	No.....	9%	Free (A,CA,E,IL,J, MX)	45%
8204.20.00	00	Socket wrenches, with or without handles, drives and extensions, and parts thereof......	X.......	9%	Free (A,CA,E,IL,J, MX)	45%
8205		Handtools (including glass cutters) not elsewhere specified or included; blow torches and similar self-contained torches; vises, clamps and the like, other than accessories for and parts of machine tools; anvils; portable forges; hand- or pedal-operated grinding wheels with frameworks; base metal parts thereof:				
8205.10.00	00	Drilling, threading or tapping tools, and parts thereof...............................	X.......	6.2%	Free (A,CA,E,IL,J, MX)	45%
8205.20		Hammers and sledge hammers, and parts thereof:				
8205.20.30	00	With heads not over 1.5 kg each..........	doz.....	6.2%	Free (A,CA,E,IL,J, MX)	45%
8205.20.60	00	With heads over 1.5 kg each..............	doz.....	Free		20%
8205.30		Planes, chisels, gouges and similar cutting tools for working wood, and parts thereof:				
8205.30.30	00	With cutting part containing by weight over 0.2 percent of chromium, molybdenum, or tungsten or over 0.1 percent of vanadium................................	X.......	5.7%	Free (A,CA,E,IL,J, MX)	60%
8205.30.60	00	Other (including parts).................	X.......	5%	Free (A,CA,E,IL,J, MX)	45%

ENTRY SUMMARY

Form Approved OMB No. 1515-0065

209
R.G. Hobelmann & Co., Inc.
24 Drayton Street
Suite 920/Realty Building
Savannah, Ga. 31402

① Entry No. C15-7654321-0	② Entry Type Code 01	3. Entry Summary Date
4. Entry Date 022689	⑤ Port Code 1703	031289
6. Bond No. 891	7. Bond Type Code 9	8. Broker/Importer File No. 44/046470

9. Ultimate Consignee Name and Address

10. Consignee No.

⑪ Importer of Record Name and Address
Allchem Industries, Inc.
4001 Newberry Rd., E-3
Gainesville, Fl. 32607

⑫ Importer No. 59-219864300

⑬ Exporting Country TW

14. Export Date 012689

⑮ Country of Origin TW

16. Missing Documents

FL
State

⑰ I.T. No.

⑱ I.T. Date

⑲ B/L or AWB No. KEESAVA001

20. Mode of Transportation 11

21. Manufacturer I.D.

22. Reference No.

㉓ Importing Carrier Ming Universe

24. Foreign Port of Lading 58301

25. Location of Goods/G.O. No.

26. U.S. Port of Unlading 1703

㉗ Import Date 022289

GCT Cont Central

㉘ Line No	30 (A) T.S.U.S.A. No. (B) ADA/CVD Case No.	31. (A) Gross Weight (B) Manifest Qty.	㉙ Description of Merchandise	㉜ Net Quantity in T.S.U.S.A. Units	33 (A) Entered Value (B) CHGS (C) Relationship	34 (A) T.S.U.S.A. Rate (B) ADA/CVD Rate (C) I.R.C. Rate (D) Visa No.	㉟ Duty and I.R. Tax Dollars	Cents
001	CPDS Triazine Ring, NSPF 2933.69.00	123901	Invoice 1 118000 LBS		N 74416 C5945	3.5%	2604	56
	81361.00 at 1,000,0000R Inv. Value DED/MMV NDC Ent Value	81361 US Cy. 6945 74416						

㊱ Declaration of Importer of Record (Owner or Purchaser) or Authorized Agent

I declare that I am the
☐ importer of record and that the actual owner, purchaser, or consignee for customs purposes is as shown above. OR ☒ owner or purchaser or agent thereof.

I further declare that the merchandise
☒ was obtained pursuant to a purchase or agreement to purchase and that the prices set forth in the invoice are true. OR ☐ was not obtained pursuant to a purchase or agreement to purchase and the statements in the invoice as to value or price are true to the best of my knowledge and belief.

I also declare that the statements in the documents herein filed fully disclose to the best of my knowledge and belief the true prices, values, quantities, rebates, drawbacks, fees, commissions, and royalties and are true and correct, and that all goods or services provided to the seller of the merchandise either free or at reduced cost are fully disclosed. I will immediately furnish to the appropriate customs officer any information showing a different state of facts.

Notice required by Paperwork Reduction Act of 1980: This information is needed to ensure that importers/exporters are complying with U.S. customs laws, to allow us to compute and collect the right amount of money, to enforce other agency requirements, and to collect accurate statistical information on imports. Your response is mandatory.

↓ U.S. CUSTOMS USE ↓

		TOTALS	
A. Liq. Code	B. Ascertained Duty	㊲ Duty	2604	56
	C. Ascertained Tax	㊳ Tax	
	D. Ascertained Other	㊴ Other	
	E. Ascertained Total	㊵ Total	2604	56

㊶ Signature of Declarant, Title and Date
R.G. Hobelmann & Co., Inc., As Agent   3/12/89

PART 1 — RECORD COPY

Customs Form 7501 (030684)

Pincotta Sales Ltd

INVOICE

MARKS AND NUMBERS
DC 1-10 MADE IN SPAIN

To

**Checkmate INc.
600 Pawn Drive
Brunswick, GA. 31520**

Date	**1/30/85**
Invoice No.	**1299**
P.O. No.	**123652**
Vendor No.	**6450**
	Ex-Works
Terms	**5 days after shipping via T/TRANSFER**
Payment Due	**Upon fax of ocean bill of lading**

Description	Part No.	Quantity	Price	Amount
Chess Boards	**346**	**240**	**$3.00**	**$720.00**
				$0.00
				$0.00
				$0.00
				$0.00
			Subtotal	**$720.00**
			Shipping	**$0.00**
			Tax	**0.00%**
			TOTAL	**$720.00**

PRO FORMA INVOICE

Importers Statement of Value or the Price Paid in the Form of an Invoice

Not being in possession of a special or commercial seller's or shipper's invoice I request that you accept the statement of value or the the price paid in the form of an invoice submitted below:

Name of shipper __Pincotta Sales Ltd.__ address __#12 Rio ORO, Madrid Spain__

Name of seller __Same__ address _____

Name of consignee __Checkmate Inc.__ address __7600 Pawn Dr. Brunswick Ga. 31520__

Name of purchaser __Same__ address _____

The merchandise (has) (has not) been purchased or agreed to be purchased by me. The prices, or in the case of consigned goods the values, given below are true and correct to the best of my knowledge and belief, and are based upon (check basis with an "X"):

(a) The prices paid or agreed to be paid (x) as per order dated __1/30/85__

(d) Knowledge of the market in the country of exporta-tion (   )

(b) Advices from exporter by letter (   ) by cable (   ) dated _____

(e) Knowledge of the market in the United States (if U.S. value) (   )

(c) Comparative values of shipments previously received (   ) dated _____

(f) Advices of the District Director of Customs (   )

(g) Other (   )

A	B	C	D	E	F	G
Case marks numbers	Manufac-turer's item number symbol or brand	Quantities and full description	Unit purchase price (currency)	Total purchase price (currency)	Unit foreign value	Total foreign value
DC 1-10	346	240 Chess Boards	$3.00	$720		

Check which of the charges below are, and which are not, included in the prices listed in columns "D" and "E":

	Amount	Included	Not included		Amount	Included	Not included
Packing		x		Lighterage			x
Cartage		x		Ocean freight			x
Inland freight		x		U.S. duties			x
Wharfage and loading abroad		x		Other charges (identify by name and amount)			x
Country of origin Spain				Total			

If any other invoice is received, I will immediately file it with the District Director of Customs.

Date __Today__   Signature of person making invoice __Shelly Kosar__

Title and firm name __Owner Checkmate Inc.__

DEPARTMENT OF THE TREASURY
UNITED STATES CUSTOMS SERVICE

OMB No. 1515-0068; 03/31/86

REQUEST FOR INFORMATION

General Information (Instructions on reverse)

19 U.S.C. 1481, 1499,
1500, 1508, and 1509

1. DATE OF REQUEST
4/7/89

2. DATE OF ENTRY & IMPORTATION
2/3/89

MANUFACTURER/SELLER/SHIPPER	4. CARRIER	5. ENTRY NO.
J. Van Zed & Zn.N.V.	Trans World Airlines	C15-1234567-0

A. INVOICE DESCRIPTION OF MERCHANDISE	6B. INVOICE NO.	7. TSUS ITEM NO.
Diamond Styli	3	8522.90.90

8. COUNTRY OF ORIGIN/EXPORTATION	9. CUSTOMHOUSE BROKER AND REFERENCE OR FILE NO.
Holland	Overseas Enterprises 81-3006

0. TO	11. FROM:
XYZ Corporation 1283 Creed Road North Atlanta, Georgia 30308	Port Director U.S. Customs Service 699 Piedmont Avenue, NE Atlanta, Georgia 30308

PRODUCTION OF DOCUMENTS AND/OR INFORMATION REQUIRED BY LAW: If you have provided the information requested on this form to U.S. Customs at other ports, please indicate the port of entry to which it was supplied, and furnish a copy of your reply to this office, if possible.	A. PORT	B. DATE INFORMATION FURNISHED

12. PLEASE ANSWER INDICATED QUESTION(S)	13. PLEASE FURNISH INDICATED ITEM(S)
A. Are you related (see reverse) in any way to the seller of this merchandise? If you are related, please describe the relationship, and explain how this relationship affects the price paid or payable for the merchandise.	[X] A. Copy of contract (or purchase order and seller's confirmation thereof) covering this transaction, and any revisions thereto.
[X] B. Identify and give details of any additional costs/expenses incurred in this transaction, such as:	[X] B. Descriptive or illustrative literature or information explaining what the merchandise is, where and how it is used, and exactly how it operates.
[X] (1) packing	C. Breakdown of component materials or ingredients by weight and the actual cost of the components at the time of assembly into the finished article.
[X] (2) commissions	D. Submit samples: Article no. and description _____
[X] (3) proceeds that accrue to the seller (see reverse)	from container no. _____
[X] (4) assists (see reverse)	mark(s) and no. _____ Samples consumed in analysis, and other samples whose return is not specifically requested, will not normally be returned.
[X] (5) royalties and/or license fees (see reverse)	[X] E. See Item 14, below.

14. CUSTOMS OFFICER MESSAGE

1. Should any contracts or agreements apply to this purchase, other than those requested about, please supply copies of these agreements.

2. Should any payment have been made to the manufacturer, seller or a third party other than those specified on the invoice, please describe these payments in full. You should include to whom such payment was made, the purpose of the payment and the amount of the payment.

15. REPLY MESSAGE (Please print or type. Use additional sheets if more space is needed.)

16. CERTIFICATION	It is required that an appropriate corporate/company official execute this certificate and/or endorse all correspondence in response to the information requested (NOTE: NOT REQUIRED IF FOREIGN FIRM COMPLETES THIS FORM).		
I hereby certify that the information furnished herewith or upon this form in response to this inquiry is true and correct, and that any samples provided were taken from the shipment covered by this entry.	A. NAME AND TITLE/POSITION OF SIGNER (Owner, Importer, or Corporate/Company Official - Print or Type)	B. SIGNATURE	
		C. TELEPHONE NO.	D. DATE

17. CUSTOMS OFFICER (Print or Type)	18. TEAM DESIGNATION	19. TELEPHONE NO.
Import Specialist	CST-01	(404) 881-4965

(Paperwork Reduction Act Notice on reverse)

Customs Form 28 (070984)

ORIGINAL

90

GENERAL INFORMATION AND INSTRUCTIONS

1 The requested information is necessary for proper classification and/or appraisement of your merchandise and/or for insuring import compliance of such merchandise. Your reply is required in accordance with section 509(a), Tariff Act of 1930, as amended (19 U.S.C. 1509).

2 All information, documents, and samples requested must relate to the shipment of merchandise described on the front of this form.

3 Please answer all indicated questions to the best of your knowledge.

4 All information submitted will be treated confidentially.

5 If a reply cannot be made within 30 days from the date of this request or if you wish to discuss any of the questions designated for your reply, please contact the Customs officer whose name appears on the front of this form.

6 Return a copy of this form with your reply.

DEFINITIONS OF KEY WORDS IN BLOCK 12.

Question A. RELATED — The persons specified below shall be treated as persons who are related:

(A) Members of the same family, including brothers and sisters (whether by whole or half blood), spouse, ancestors, and lineal descendants.

(B) Any officer or director of an organization and such organization.

(C) An officer or director of an organization and an officer or director of another organization, if each such individual is also an officer or director in the other organization.

(D) Partners.

(E) Employer and employee.

(F) Any person directly or indirectly owning, controlling, or holding with power to vote, 5 percent or more of the outstanding voting stock or shares of any organization and such organization.

(G) Two or more persons directly or indirectly controlling, controlled by or under common control with, any person.

PRICE PAID OR PAYABLE — This term is defined as the total payment (whether direct or indirect, and exclusive of any costs, charges, or expenses incurred for transportation, insurance, and other C.I.F. charges) made, or to be made, for imported merchandise by the buyer to, or for the benefit of, the seller.

Question B. ASSISTS — The term "assist" means any of the following if supplied directly or indirectly, and free of charge or at reduced cost, by the buyer of the imported merchandise for use in connection with the production or the sale for export to the United States of the merchandise:

(1) Materials, components, parts, and similar items incorporated in the imported merchandise.

(2) Tools, dies, molds, and similar items used in the production of the imported merchandise.

(3) Merchandise consumed in the production of the imported merchandise.

(4) Engineering, development, artwork, design work, and plans and sketches that are undertaken elsewhere than in the United States and are necessary for the production of the imported merchandise.

PROCEEDS THAT ACCRUE TO THE SELLER — This term is defined as the amount of any subsequent resale, disposal, or use of the imported merchandise that accrues, directly or indirectly, to the seller.

ROYALTIES AND/OR LICENSE FEES — This term relates to those amounts that the buyer is required to pay, directly, or indirectly, as a condition of the sale of the imported merchandise for exportation to the United States.

NOTICE OF ACTION				
	NOTICE OF ACTION *This is NOT a Notice of Liquidation*			1 DATE OF THIS NOTICE 5/15/89
2 CARRIER TWA	3 DATE OF IMPORTATION 2/2/89	4 DATE OF ENTRY 2/3/89		5 ENTRY NO C15-1234567-0
6 MFR/SELLER/SHIPPER J. Van Zed & ZN.N.V.	7 COUNTRY Holland	8 CUSTOMHOUSE BROKER AND FILE NO Overseas Enterprises 89-3006		

9 DESCRIPTION OF MERCHANDISE

Diamond Styli

10 TO	11 FROM
XYZ Corporation 1283 Creek Road North Atlanta, Georgia 30308	Port Director U.S. Customs Service 699 Piedmont Avenue, NE Atlanta, Georgia 30308

12 THE FOLLOWING ACTION, WHICH WILL RESULT IN AN INCREASE IN DUTIES,—

[ ] IS **PROPOSED.** IF YOU DISAGREE WITH THIS PROPOSED ACTION, PLEASE FURNISH YOUR REASONS IN WRITING TO THIS OFFICE WITHIN 20 DAYS FROM THE DATE OF THIS NOTICE. AFTER 20 DAYS THE ENTRY WILL BE LIQUIDATED AS PROPOSED.

[X] HAS BEEN **TAKEN.** THE ENTRY IS IN THE LIQUIDATION PROCESS AND IS NOT AVAILABLE FOR REVIEW IN THIS OFFICE.

TYPE OF ACTION

A. [X] RATE ADVANCE

B. [ ] VALUE ADVANCE

C. [ ] EXCESS [ ] WEIGHT [ ] QUANTITY

D. [ ] OTHER *(See below)*

13 EXPLANATION *(Refer to Action letter designations above)*

As these styli (needles) are designed for and intended for use with video disc players only, and are sufficiently manufactured at the time of importation as to be considered dedicated to this use and capable of no others, than they would be considered parts of the video disc players. Therefore, the correct classification is 8522.90.90/3.9%, as parts of television apparatus.

14 CUSTOMS OFFICER *(Print or Type)* Import Specialist	15 TEAM DESIGNATION CST-1	16 TELEPHONE (404)881-4956

DEPARTMENT OF THE TREASURY
U.S. CUSTOMS SERVICE
152.2 C. R.

CUSTOMS FORM 29
(2-1-79)

ORIGINAL (WHITE) - IMPORTER

REFER INQUIRIES TO:

U. S. CUSTOMS SERVICE

District Director
Post Office Building
Pembina, North Dakota 58271

GOODS ENTERED AT:

Portal, North Dakota

COURTESY NOTICE

ENTRIES SCHEDULED TO LIQUIDATE

SERIES	TYPE AND ENTRY NO	DATE OF ENTRY	LIQUID COOL	INITIAL AMOUNT	LIQUIDATION AMOUNT
83	C 405721-6	11/12/82	401	1200.84	1475.14

IMPORTER NUMBER	DATE OF LIQUIDATION
12-4017612	3/04/83

* INDICATES REFUND TO DIFFERENT ADDRESS
* INDICATES OFFSET OF REFUNDS

Your entry is scheduled to liquidate on the date indicated for the liquidation amount. Any difference between this amount and the initial amount paid will be billed or refunded to you.
If you are dissatisfied with the liquidated amount, a protest may be filed within 90 days of the date of liquidation according to the procedures set forth in Part 174 of the Customs Regulations (19 CFR Part 174).

DEPARTMENT OF THE TREASURY
U.S. CUSTOMS SERVICE
CUSTOMS FORM 4333A (05 2881)

93

DEPARTMENT OF THE TREASURY
I.S. CUSTOMS SERVICE
34.51,134 52,141.113,C.R.

NOTICE OF REDELIVERY—MARKINGS, ETC.

PORT	ENTRY NO.	DATE OF ENTRY	No. of Cases Released
			0
			No. of Cases Retained
Chicago	C.E. C15-7654321-0	7/18/89	2

MARKETING STATUTE, ETC.			FROM (Include Phone No.)
XX Section 304, T.A.	☐ Fur Products Labeling Act	☐ Other	James R. Sands
☐ Wool Products Labeling Act	☐ Foreign Assets Control Regulations		District Director
☐ Schedule 7, Part 2E Headnote 4 TSUSA	X Textile Fiber Products Identification Act		610 S. Canal Street Chicago, Il 60607 (312) 363-6100

W.R. Zanes
223 N. Orleans Street
Chicago, Il 60666

For the account of ABC Imports

TO IMPORTER—Redelivery is hereby ordered of the following shipment for the reason stated above. Deliver to Customs all merchandise which has been released to you under the terms of the entry bond. This shipment can not be released unless brought into conformity with the statute indicated. Articles not returned or properly marked within 30 days of this notice become liable for liquidated damage.

DESCRIPTION OF MERCHANDISE	QUANTITY	MARKS—NUMBERS
Woven Wearing Apparel (ladies' blouses) Cotton 24 pcs. per carton 6206.30.30 - 16.4% Brunswick International Airways AWB 023-8769-4780	2 cartons	ABC/1-2

☐ You are authorized to mark the merchandise at a place other than public stores. When marking is accomplished complete certification below and return both copies of this form ☐ with ☐ without a sample of the marked merchandise of this office. Merchandise must be held until marking is verified or notification received that marking is acceptable.

☒ Merchandise to be marked under customs supervision.
X

REMARKS:
Goods are to be marked with the fiber content (100% cotton) and the country of origin
(Made in France)

SIGNATURE OF CUSTOM OFFICER		DATE
[signature] District Director		7/18/89

IMPORTER—COMPLETE APPROPRIATE ITEMS

	Place	Date	Time
☐ Merchandise is to be marked at place other than Public Stores.			
☐ Merchandise to be ☐ exported ☐ destroyed under customs supervision in lieu of marking. I (we) guarantee the payment of all expenses incident to above action.	Place	Date	Time

☐ I certify that the merchandise has been marked to indicate the country of origin as required by Section 304, Tariff Act 1930.
Sample ☐ is ☐ is not submitted herewith.

SIGNATURE OF IMPORTER	DATE

☐ _____: Supervise the required action as set forth in this notice.

☐ Marking waived pursuant to your request dated _____
☐ The merchandise has been ☐ legally marked ☐ exported ☐ destroyed or, ☐ the certified marking accepted, except as noted on reverse.

SIGNATURE OF CUSTOMS OFFICER	DATE

(Previous editions may be used)   Customs Form 4647 (082083)

ORIGINAL

94

EXCEPTIONS TO MARKING REQUIREMENTS

While most imported merchandise is subject to marking requirements (showing conspicuously, permanently and indelibly the country of origin in English), certain items can be exempted from marking. If an importer believes his import does not have to be marked he is encouraged to verify his opinion with U.S. Customs. It is always much easier and less expensive to have merchandise marked overseas at time of manufacture than after the fact in the United States.

Some examples (taken from 19CFR 134.32) of ways that a product could be exempt from marking are:

1-   Articles incapable of being marked.
2-   Articles that cannot be marked prior to shipment to the U.S. without injury.
3-   Articles that cannot be marked prior to shipment to the U.S. except at an expense economically prohibitive of its importation.
4-   Articles that the marking of the containers will reasonably indicate its origin.
5-   Articles which are crude substances.
6-   Articles imported for use exclusively by the importer, NOT FOR RESALE!
7-   Articles that would be further processed in the U.S. by or for the importer, that any mark would be obliterated, destroyed or permanently concealed.
8-   Articles that the ultimate purchaser would necessarily know the country of origin.
9-   Articles produced more than 20 years prior to importation.
10-   Articles imported, or withdrawn from warehouse, to be immediately exported.
11-   Products of American fisheries which are free of duty.
12-   Products of possessions of the United States.
13-   Products of the U.S. exported and returned.
14-   Certain NAFTA products (from Canada or Mexico, check with Customs).

Marking can also be waived on import if the import re-packs the articles and in re-packing marks the article with the country of origin. This if often done with shrink-wrapping.

While the above items indicate many instances where marking can be exempted by Customs, for Country of origin purposes, it should never be taken for granted that marking is waived automatically.

The above list, while abridged from the Code of Federal Regulations, is not inclusive, and importers are encouraged to research each prospective import in advance of purchase.

DEPARTMENT OF THE TREASURY
U.S. CUSTOMS SERVICE
132.22, 132.23, C.R., 9.4, 9.11, C.M.

NOTICE TO ADDRESSEE OF ARRIVAL OF MAIL SHIPMENT

PARCEL ADDRESSED TO:

John Smith
Atlanta, Ga.

John Smith
1283 Peachtree Place
Atlanta, Georgia 30309

DISTRICT NO.
17

PORT OF
03 (Atlanta)

DATE OF THIS NOTICE
071389

NO. OF PACKAGES
1

PACKAGE NOS.
As Addr.

COUNTRY OF ORIGIN
England

DESCRIPTION OF CONTENTS

3 Figurines and 2 steins

NAME AND ADDRESS OF FOREIGN SHIPPER

Van Dam Art Shop, London, England

DATE OF EXPORTATION

063089

THE ABOVE SHIPMENT IS BEING HELD FOR FORMAL CUSTOMS ENTRY FOR THE FOLLOWING REASONS:

- [X] Value over $250 ($1500.00)
- [ ] No value shown
- [ ] Proper Customs Administration (Where Formal Entry is required regardless of value)

IF THIS IS A COMMERCIAL SHIPMENT VALUED OVER $250, the addressee or his duly authorized agent or transferee should present this notice (in lieu of bill of lading) together with invoice and appropriate entry papers to:

Port Director
699 Piedmont Avenue, N.E.
Atlanta, Ga. 30308

Commercial Shipments valued in excess of $250 require formal customs entry

IF THIS IS A NONCOMMERCIAL SHIPMENT VALUED AT OVER $250, not imported for sale or on commission, but imported for the personal or household use of you or your family, return this notice to Port Director of Customs, Atlanta, Ga. 30308 with an explaining letter and any supporting documents. If the actual value of your shipment is not shown above, please attach invoice to this notice.

ADDRESSEE

- [ ] Check here if you desire formal appraisement of this shipment. Otherwise this mail shipment will be released to you under a mail entry for delivery to you by the postal service upon payment of any duties and taxes found due by Customs.

IF THE ACTUAL VALUE OF THIS SHIPMENT IS $250 OR LESS, mail invoices, bills of lading and any other supporting documents with this notice to the undersigned at

The U.S. Postal Service charges a Clearance and Delivery fee on all dutiable parcels. Storage charges will begin accruing on the sixth working day following the date of this notice.

SIGNATURE OF CUSTOMS OFFICER [signature]

DATE 7/5/89

CUSTOMS FORM 3509 (1-14-76)

ADDRESSEE

If entry is to be made by someone other than the addressee this notice must be endorsed by the addressee

DEPARTMENT OF THE TREASURY UNITED STATES CUSTOMS SERVICE	Case Number 89-3901-55678

NOTICE OF PENALTY OR LIQUIDATED DAMAGES INCURRED

AND DEMAND FOR PAYMENT

19 CFR 1R 6, 172.31

Port Name and Code
Chicago, Il 3901
Investigation File No.

TO:
W.R. Jones & Co.
For Account of ABC Imports
223 N. Orleans Street
Chicago, Il 60666

IRS# - 13-5567855

DEMAND IS HEREBY MADE FOR PAYMENT OF $ __131.20__ , representing ☐ Penalties or ☒ Liquidated Damages
assessed against you for violation of law or regulation, or breach of bond, as set forth below:

Consumption Entry Summary C-15-5476271-1 was submitted on June 7, 1989 to cover
2 cartons of ladies silk blouses, woven, not ornamented (6206.30.30, 16.4%) which
arrived on June 1, 1989 from Paris France on Brunswick International Airways,
AWB 023-8769-4781, and was consigned to ABC Imports. Original invoices submitted
totalled $200, duty was $32.80. Upon examination, invoices totalling $400 were
discovered. Correct amount of duty equals $65.60. Loss of revenue amounted to
$32.80. Penalty assessed for gross negligence equals 4 times loss of revenue or
$131.20.

LAW OR REGULATION VIOLATED	BOND BREACHED
19 USC 1592	Importer's Bond

DESCRIPTION OF BOND (if any)	Form Number CF 301	Amount $100,000	Date Continuous

Name and Address of Principal in Bond
W.R. Jones & Co., 223 N. Orleans St., Chicago, Il 60666

Name and Address of Surety on Bond	Surety Identification No.
All American Insurance Co., P.O. Box 1980, New York, New York 12234	231

If you feel there are extenuating circumstances, you have the right to object to the above action. Your petition should explain why you
should not be penalized for the cited violation. Write the petition as a letter or in legal form; submit in (duplicate) (triplicate),
addressed to the Commissioner of Customs, and forward to the District Director of Customs at

P.O. Box 0000, Chicago, Illinois 60606

Unless the amount herein demanded is paid or a petition for relief is filed with the district director of customs within the indicated time limit, further action will be taken in connection with your bond or the matter will be referred to the United States Attorney.	TIME LIMIT FOR PAYMENT OR FILING PETITION FOR RELIEF (Days from the date of this Notice)	30

Signature By	Title District Director	Date 6/30/89

Customs Form 5955A (012386)

97

Form approved OMB No. 1515-0056

DEPARTMENT OF THE TREASURY
UNITED STATES CUSTOMS SERVICE
PROTEST
Pursuant to Sections 514 &515(a), Tariff Act of 1930
as amended, 19 CFR 174 et seq.

1. PROTEST NO. *(Supplied by Customs)*
89-17013000019

2. DATE RECEIVED *(Customs Use Only)*
07/01/89

NOTE: If your protest is denied, in whole or in part, and you wish to CONTEST the denial, you may do so by bringing a civil action in the U.S. Court of International Trade within 180 days after the date of mailing of Notice of Denial. You may obtain further information concerning the institution of an action by writing the Clerk of U.S. Court of International Trade, One Federal Plaza, New York, New York 10007. (212) 264-2800)

SECTION I — IMPORTER AND ENTRY IDENTIFICATION

3. DISTRICT	4. IMPORTER NO.
Savannah	86-4039198

6. NAME AND ADDRESS OF IMPORTER OR OTHER PROTESTING PARTY

Audio Distributers, Inc.
1234 George Street
Savannah, Ga. 31401

5. ENTRY DETAILS

PORT CODE	FY	ENTRY NO	CHECK DIGIT	DATE OF ENTRY	DATE OF LIQUIDATION
01	89	C15-1234567	0	02/03/89	06/07/89

SECTION II — APPLICATION FOR FURTHER REVIEW
(Fill in Item 1 above if this is a separate Application for Further Review.)

7. ☐ THIS IS AN APPLICATION FOR FURTHER REVIEW IN LIEU OF REVIEW BY THE DISTRICT DIRECTOR. *(Complete Item 8 below.)*

☐ YES ☐ NO 8. Please answer each of the following questions as these criteria must be met for approval of further review of protest, IF REQUESTED ABOVE.

Have you made prior request of a district director for a further review of the same claim with respect to the same or substantially similar merchandise?

Have you received a final adverse decision from the U.S. Court of Int'l Trade on the same claim with respect to the same category of merchandise before the do you have action involving such a claim pending before the U.S. Court of International Trade?

Have you previously received an adverse administrative decision from the Commissioner of Customs or his designee or have you presently pending an application for an administrative decision on the same claim with respect to the same category of merchandise?

SECTION III — DETAILED REASONS FOR PROTEST AND/OR FURTHER REVIEW

9. With respect to each category of merchandise, set forth, separately, (1) each decision protested, (2) the claim of the protesting party, and (3) the factual material and legal arguments which are believed to support the protest. All such material and arguments should be specific. General statements of conclusions are not sufficient. If Further Review is applied for, set forth, additionally, a justification for Further Review under the criteria in 19 CFR 174.24 and 174.25.

The imported diamond tone arm styli (needles) were classified as parts of tone arms under HTSUS 8529.10.60/6%.

We believe that the merchandise is properly considered to be parts of television apparatus as they are used only on video disc players. Therefore, they would be properly classified at 8522.90.90/3.9%.

(Attach Additional Sheets, If Necessary)

SECTION IV — SIGNATURE AND MAILING INSTRUCTIONS

10. NAME AND ADDRESS OF PERSON TO WHOM ANY NOTICE OF APPROVAL OR DENIAL SHOULD BE SENT

John Williams
Audio Distributers, Inc.
1234 George Street
Savannah, Ga. 31401

11. IF FILING AS ATTORNEY OR AGENT, TYPE OR PRINT YOUR NAME. ADDRESS, AND IMPORTER NO., IF ANY

OVERSEAS Customs Brokers, Inc.
912 Bay Street
Savannah, Ga. 31401   42-6092156

12. SIGNATURE AND DATE
(signature) 7/1/89

SECTION V — DECISION (CUSTOMS USE ONLY)

13. THIS ☐ PROTEST ☐ APPLICATION FOR FURTHER REVIEW HAS BEEN:

☐ DENIED IN FULL OR IN PART BECAUSE ☐ APPROVED *

☐ Untimely Filed

☐ See attached protest review decision

☐ Does not meet criteria

☐ Other, namely ⟶

* When further review only is approved, the decision on the protest is suspended, pending issuance of a protest review decision.

14. TITLE OF CUSTOMS OFFICER	15. SIGNATURE	DATE
PROTEST CLERK	*(signature)*	7/11/89

PAPERWORK REDUCTION ACT OF 1980 STATEMENT: The U.S. Customs Service requires the information in this form to ensure compliance with Customs laws, to identify documents and statements in order to allow or deny the protest, and to advise protestant. Your response is required to obtain a benefit.

EDITIONS PRIOR TO 090883 ARE OBSOLETE.

Customs Form 19 (121686)

LANDED COST WORKSHEET

Importer's should calculate landed cost before actually importing any product to be assured that they can do so profitably. A worksheet, similar to the below form should be used. It is stressed that importers should be sure they have the correct packing specifications of their intended import (weight, size, pallets, container, etc.) to enable them to secure freight rates. What costs to add in above the purchase price is contingent on the terms of sale, be guided accordingly.

Item- 100 stainless steel sink	$45.00	$50.00	$60.00	$80.00
Terms of sale-	**Ex-works**	**FOB**	**CIF**	**CIFDDP**
Invoice value	$4500.00	$5000.00	$6000.00	$8000.00
Foreign export license	100.00	included	included	included
Independent inspection	100.00	100.00	100.00	100.00
Export packing	included	included	included	included
Transport to foreign port	250.00	included	included	included
Foreign port charges	100.00	included	included	included
Loading on vessel	50.00	included	included	included
International freight	1200.00	1200.00	included	included
Terminal charges / U.S.	400.00	400.00	400.00	included
U.S. Customs Duty/fees	168.08	186.75	178.16	included
U.S. Custom broker fee	100.00	100.00	100.00	included
Loading/U.S.	180.00	180.00	180.00	included
U.S. Customs Inspection	150.00	150.00	150.00	included
Delivery to door in U.S.	250.00	250.00	250.00	included
Insurance	30.00	30.00	included	included
Total	$7578.08	$7596.75	$7358.16	$8100.00
Cost per sink-	$75.78	$75.97	$73.58	$81.00

The above workup is fictional but should illustrate the type of worksheet that each importer should create BEFORE actually purchasing cargo. This workup assumes that the importer has a yearly bond eliminating any bond costs. Inspection overseas is optional. Inspection in the U.S. is not mandatory but possible. It is always better to overestimate the landed cost than under estimate.